Conditionally Accepted

Conditionally Accepted

~

*Christians' Perspectives on Sexuality
and Gay and Lesbian Civil Rights*

BAKER A. ROGERS

Rutgers University Press

New Brunswick, Camden, and Newark, New Jersey, and London

Library of Congress Cataloging-in-Publication Data

Names: Rogers, Baker A., author.
Title: Conditionally accepted : Christians' perspectives on sexuality
and gay and lesbian civil rights / Baker A. Rogers.
Description: New Brunswick : Rutgers University Press, 2019. |
Includes bibliographical references and index.
Identifiers: LCCN 2019010256 | ISBN 9781978805019 (hardback) |
ISBN 9781978805002 (pbk.)
Subjects: LCSH: Sex—Religious aspects—Christianity. |
Homosexuality—Religious aspects—Christianity. | Sexual rights.
Classification: LCC BT708 .R564 2019 | DDC 233/.5—dc23
LC record available at https://lccn.loc.gov/2019010256

A British Cataloging-in-Publication record for this book is
available from the British Library.

∞ The paper used in this publication meets the requirements of the American
National Standard for Information Sciences—Permanence of Paper for Printed
Library Materials, ANSI Z39.48-1992.

www.rutgersuniversitypress.org

Manufactured in the United States of America

I dedicate this work to all lesbian, gay, bisexual, transgender, and otherwise queer individuals who have struggled to accept themselves due to religious teachings and to all the religious leaders who stand for equality and love.

Contents

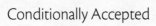

Conditionally Accepted

Introduction

ME: Hi. You completed a survey indicating that you would be willing
to be interviewed. Are you still willing to complete an interview
with me?

REGINA (sixty-five-year-old white evangelical Protestant from the
Mississippi Delta): You're gay, right? I'll do the interview if you
think you can be objective.

In late September 2013, I traveled to the coast of Mississippi to
complete my first round of interviews. Gulf Coast Nondenominational Church was a small tan structure; at the road, a small
blue sign with three crosses announced that I arrived. I was led to
the children's nursery, where I was to conduct my interviews. The
morning of the interviews, I went in early to set up, and I situated
two rocking chairs: one for the participants and one for me. As I
was getting my bearings, I noticed that directly in front of me the
entire wall was painted with a scene of Noah's Ark.[1] From one side
of the painting to the other was a large rainbow, the symbolism of
which was overwhelming. As I prepared to interview Christians
about their attitudes and beliefs toward homosexuality[2] and gay
and lesbian civil rights, I was faced by a symbol that has great
meaning for both groups. For Christians, the rainbow is a symbol
of hope—a symbol of God's love and caring for them. For lesbian,
gay, bisexual, transgender, and other queer (LGBTQ) individuals,
the rainbow is a symbol of pride and unity. Despite the positive
meanings of the rainbow for both groups, these symbols seemed

worlds apart during my interviews at Gulf Coast Nondenominational Church. This particular church was not a place where
the LGBTQ pride symbol would be welcomed or accepted. This
church only welcomed gay and lesbian people with the goal of
salvation from sin, particularly the sin of homosexuality. This was a
place where gay and lesbian pride would be discouraged. The irony
of this juxtaposition is where this story begins.

By the end of 2013, I had completed forty interviews with Mississippi Christians about their religious beliefs, their views about
homosexuality, and their attitudes toward gay and lesbian civil
rights.[3] The interviewees, whose voices guide this book, repre-
sent various denominations and churches that span from the Gulf
Coast of Mississippi to the Tennessee state line, and everywhere in
between. The respondents identified with three distinct religious
traditions: evangelical Protestantism, mainline Protestantism, and
Catholicism. The history and beliefs of these distinct religious
traditions guided the respondents in this book to very different
conclusions about homosexuality and gay and lesbian rights today,
making it necessary to discuss each tradition more fully before
moving forward.

Evangelical Protestants, Mainline Protestants, and Catholics

Evangelical Protestantism, as we know it today, began in the 1920s
and encompasses multiple Protestant denominations. Currently,
about one out of every four Christians in the United States identifies as an evangelical Protestant (Pew Forum 2014). The hallmarks
of evangelical Protestantism include the belief that the Bible does
not contain errors, which often leads evangelicals to call for a literal interpretation of the Bible; the belief that salvation from sins
comes only through a personal relationship with Jesus Christ; and
the belief that it is a Christian's duty to spread the Christian message (Bartkowski 2001, 2004). This means it is not a person's works
or good deeds that save them from their sinful nature and punishment; rather, a person gains salvation by accepting that Jesus died
on the cross for them and only he can save them from their sinful

nature. The belief in spreading the gospel, also known as evangeliz-
ing, is where evangelical Protestants break off from fundamentalist
Protestants. Fundamentalists believe that their job as Christians
is to live a good life and prepare for the End Times; they do not
stress the importance of spreading the message of Christianity to
others. All the conservative Protestants in this study felt they were
called to spread the gospel, which classifies them as evangelicals
rather than fundamentalists.

In contrast to evangelical Protestants, mainline Protestants
belong to churches and denominations that are more theologically
liberal. These churches and denominations are less likely to take
a literal interpretation of the Bible, less likely to believe that theology is objective fact, and more likely to minimize or erase the
differences between Christianity and other religions[4] (Smith et al.
1998). Overall, mainline Protestants seek to be accepting of differences and to emphasize a message of love and nonjudgment. This
often means that mainline Protestants' beliefs align more closely
with secular society than those of other religious traditions.

Finally, Catholicism is the largest Christian denomination in
the United States; its members account for approximately 29 percent of religiously affiliated people in the United States (Konieczny
2013). Unlike Protestants, both liberal and conservative Catholics
remain a part of the same denomination. Despite a diversity of
beliefs, Catholics do have a central set of theological tenets they
hold as the core to Catholic identity (D'Antonio, Dillon, and
Gautier 2013). For example, approximately 75 percent of Catholics
believe that Jesus's resurrection from the dead is an important belief
to them personally (D'Antonio et al. 2013). Nonetheless, Catholics
appear to be moving away from a united front, as the majority
of Catholics across the United States today do not feel that the
teaching authority of the Vatican—the governing organization of
the Catholic Church, led by the pope—is necessary for Catholic faith. The bulk of Catholics in the United States today believe
that being a good Catholic is no longer dependent on adhering
to the church's authority or hierarchy, making them more liberal
in theology (D'Antonio et al. 2013). Only about a quarter to a third of

those who identify as Catholic accept the complete authority of the church. These more conservative Catholics continue to uphold the teachings of the Vatican.

The current pope, Pope Francis, is viewed as extremely liberal by many Catholics today. Pope Francis was elected on March 13, 2013, and made his first official statement about gay and lesbian people in September of 2013. Pope Francis has moved further and further away from overt condemnation of homosexuality and gay and lesbian civil rights. This is important to keep in mind when interpreting the Catholics' responses in this study. Conservative Catholics who have historically upheld the church's conservative teachings about sexuality may have been confused in 2013 as Pope Francis began to change the position of the Catholic Church on issues of sexuality.

In this study, I use "conservative Christians" to refer to both evangelical Protestants and conservative Catholics. Generally, conservative Christians believe that either the Bible (evangelical Protestants) or the Vatican (Catholics) is the final authority on what is morally right and wrong. Based on biblical literalism or the authority of the Catholic Church, conservative Christians generally believe that homosexuality is sinful. On the contrary, more liberal Christians, both mainline Protestants and liberal Catholics, feel there is more room for interpretation of both the Bible and the teachings of the Catholic Church. Based on these more open beliefs, liberal Christians are more likely to believe that homosexuality is not sinful, or at least only sinful in certain situations. Overall, while all the respondents in this study identified as Christian, they told very different stories about their faith and God. Some believed in a vengeful God who is going to end the world due to human failings—especially the sins of gay and lesbian people. Others believed in a loving God who forgives and accepts all people. The one thing the majority of interviewees agreed on, regardless of their denomination, was that God is important in their lives and that they were sure they were doing what God would want them to.

The Interviewees

Most respondents in this study identified as white; in fact, only four out of the forty interviewees identified their race as black / African American, and no other races were represented in this sample. When it comes to religions, research shows that race matters; therefore, it is important to remember that most of this study considers the views of white Protestants and Catholics.[5] Additionally, more women than men were willing to tell me about their beliefs. In total, twenty-eight interviewees identified as women, and twelve identified as men. Table 1 provides an overview of each interviewee, including demographic information, whether they have gay or lesbian friends or family members, and their stances on issues discussed throughout the book.

The interviewees for this study were selected from thirteen churches in Mississippi that agreed to participate in this study. Finding churches in Mississippi that would participate in a study about homosexuality and gay and lesbian rights was difficult, but a couple of pastors agreed to let me sample from their congregations and were able to recommend other pastors who would participate. It was hard to get my foot in the door, but once I did, I was able to use those connections to gain access to this community of Mississippi Christians. For more detailed information about my sampling and research methods, please see the appendix.

The Location: "Thank God for Mississippi"

In the United States, there remains a substantial minority who continue to vehemently oppose equal rights for gay and lesbian citizens; the most vocal among these opponents are evangelical Protestants (Fetner 2001, 2008; Olson, Cadge, and Harrison 2006; Saucier and Cawman 2004; Sherkat, Powell-Williams, Maddox, and Mattias de Vries 2011). That opposition ranges from radical opponents—such as Fred Phelps's Westboro Baptist Church, which pickets funerals of gay individuals and holds public protests

TABLE 1. Interview Sample Characteristics

RESPONDENT	RELIGIOUS CATEGORY	GENDER	AGE	EDUCATION	MARITAL STATUS	RACE	FRIEND	FAMILY MEMBER	SAME-SEX MARRIAGE	SAME-SEX ADOPTION	INFLUENCE OF SOCIAL CONTACT
Nick	Catholic	Man	51	Some College	Married	White	Acquaintances	No	Support	Full Acceptance	A Case for Coming Out
Kelsey	Mainline Protestant	Woman	32	Master's	Married	White	Yes	No	Support	Full Acceptance	A Case for Coming Out
Leo	Mainline Protestant	Man	60	Master's	Married	White	Yes	Yes	Support	Full Acceptance	A Case for Coming Out
Gretchen	Mainline Protestant	Woman	70	Some College	Married	White	Yes	No	Support	Full Acceptance	A Case for Coming Out
Janice	Mainline Protestant	Woman	37	Bachelor's	Single	White	Yes	No	Support	Full Acceptance	A Case for Coming Out
Victor	Mainline Protestant	Man	43	Master's	Married	White	Yes	Yes	Support	Full Acceptance	A Case for Coming Out
Brenda	Catholic	Woman	44	Professional	Married	White	Yes	Yes	Not Marriage	Not Ideal	Allies & Friends
Phillip	Catholic	Man	71	Some College	Married	White	Yes	No	Not Marriage	Not Ideal	Allies & Friends
Rick	Catholic	Man	43	Professional	Married	White	Yes	No	Support	Full Acceptance	Allies & Friends
Tracy	Catholic	Woman	63	Bachelor's	Married	White	Yes	No	Not Marriage	Not Ideal	Allies & Friends

RESPONDENT	RELIGIOUS CATEGORY	GENDER	AGE	EDUCATION	MARITAL STATUS	RACE	FRIEND	FAMILY MEMBER	SAME-SEX MARRIAGE	SAME-SEX ADOPTION	INFLUENCE OF SOCIAL CONTACT
Whitney	Catholic	Woman	52	Master's	Married	White	Yes	No	Not Marriage	Not Ideal	Allies & Friends
Mandy	Catholic	Woman	40	Master's	Married	White	Yes	No	Support	Full Acceptance	Allies & Friends
Gabby	Mainline Protestant	Woman	28	Bachelor's	Single	White	Yes	Yes	Support	Full Acceptance	Allies & Friends
Isabelle	Mainline Protestant	Woman	75	Doctorate	Married	Black	Yes	No	Support	Full Acceptance	Allies & Friends
Jason	Mainline Protestant	Man	55	Master's	Married	White	Yes	Yes	Support	Full Acceptance	Allies & Friends
Marie	Mainline Protestant	Woman	69	Associate's	Divorced	White	Acquaintances	No	Support	Full Acceptance	Allies & Friends
Nancy	Mainline Protestant	Woman	50	Master's	Married	White	Yes	No	Support	Full Acceptance	Allies & Friends
Barbara	Mainline Protestant	Woman	55	Bachelor's	Divorced	White	Acquaintances	No	Support	Not Ideal	Allies & Friends
Casey	Mainline Protestant	Woman	39	Bachelor's	Married	White	Acquaintances	No	Support	Full Acceptance	Allies & Friends
Deborah	Mainline Protestant	Woman	45	Some College	Divorced	White	Yes	Yes	Support	Full Acceptance	Allies & Friends

(continued)

TABLE 1. Interview Sample Characteristics (*continued*)

RESPONDENT	RELIGIOUS CATEGORY	GENDER	AGE	EDUCATION	MARITAL STATUS	RACE	FRIEND	FAMILY MEMBER	SAME-SEX MARRIAGE	SAME-SEX ADOPTION	INFLUENCE OF SOCIAL CONTACT
Sheena	Mainline Protestant	Woman	66	Doctorate	Widowed	Black	Yes	Yes	Support	Full Acceptance	Allies & Friends
Hannah	Mainline Protestant	Woman	23	Some College	Single	White	Yes	Yes	Support	Full Acceptance	Allies and Friends
Tim	Catholic	Man	40	Some College	Married	White	No	Yes	Opposed	Not Ideal	Homosexuality is an Abomination
David	Evangelical Protestant	Man	61	Master's	Married	White	Acquaintances	No	Opposed	Complete Opposition	Homosexuality is an Abomination
Erica	Evangelical Protestant	Woman	63	Master's	Divorced	White	Yes	Yes	Opposed	Complete Opposition	Homosexuality is an Abomination
Francis	Evangelical Protestant	Woman	50	Some College	Divorced	Black	Yes	Yes	Opposed	Complete Opposition	Homosexuality is an Abomination
Angela	Evangelical Protestant	Woman	53	Bachelor's	Married	White	No	Yes	Opposed	Complete Opposition	Homosexuality is an Abomination

RESPONDENT	RELIGIOUS CATEGORY	GENDER	AGE	EDUCATION	MARITAL STATUS	RACE	FRIEND	FAMILY MEMBER	SAME-SEX MARRIAGE	SAME-SEX ADOPTION	INFLUENCE OF SOCIAL CONTACT
Regina	Evangelical Protestant	Woman	65	Some College	Married	White	Acquaintances	Yes	Not Marriage	Complete Opposition	Homosexuality is an Abomination
Darlene	Evangelical Protestant	Woman	26	Some College	Married	White	Yes	Yes	Support	Complete Opposition	Homosexuality is an Abomination
Ervin	Mainline Protestant	Man	55	Master's	Married	Black	Yes	Yes	Not Marriage	Complete Opposition	Homosexuality is an Abomination
Wendy	Mainline Protestant	Woman	53	Bachelor's	Married	White	Yes	No	Not Marriage	Not Ideal	Homosexuality is an Abomination
Susan	Catholic	Woman	60	Bachelor's	Married	White	Yes	No	Not Marriage	Not Ideal	Love the Sinner, Hate the Sin
Hillary	Catholic	Woman	53	Master's	Married	White	Yes	Yes	Not Marriage	Not Ideal	Love the Sinner, Hate the Sin
Kristina	Catholic	Woman	36	Some College	Married	White	Yes	Yes	Opposed	Not Ideal	Love the Sinner, Hate the Sin

(continued)

TABLE 1. Interview Sample Characteristics (*continued*)

RESPONDENT	RELIGIOUS CATEGORY	GENDER	AGE	EDUCATION	MARITAL STATUS	RACE	FRIEND	FAMILY MEMBER	SAME-SEX MARRIAGE	SAME-SEX ADOPTION	INFLUENCE OF SOCIAL CONTACT
Andrew	Evangelical Protestant	Man	?	Master's	Married	White	Yes	No	Opposed	Complete Opposition	Love the Sinner, Hate the Sin
Candace	Evangelical Protestant	Woman	60	Bachelor's	Married	White	Yes	No	Opposed	Complete Opposition	Love the Sinner, Hate the Sin
Lauren	Evangelical Protestant	Woman	43	Bachelor's	Married	White	Yes	No	Not Marriage	Not Ideal	Love the Sinner, Hate the Sin
Caleb	Evangelical Protestant	Man	26	Associate's	Married	White	Yes	Yes	Support	Not Ideal	Love the Sinner, Hate the Sin
Paula	Mainline Protestant	Woman	66	Master's	Married	White	Acquaintances	No	Not Marriage	Full Acceptance	Love the Sinner, Hate the Sin
Brad	Mainline Protestant	Man	56	High School Diploma	Married	White	Yes	No	Opposed	Full Acceptance	Love the Sinner, Hate the Sin

with signs that read "God hates fags" and "Death penalty for fags"—to relatively more moderate Christian organizations such as Concerned Women for America, whose brochures promote "traditional" marriage between a man and a woman (Fetner 2001, 2008; Schreiber 2008). Despite this vocal minority, there has been a clear attitudinal shift toward acceptance of gay and lesbian rights in the United States over the past couple of decades. Nevertheless, the South has continued to stand out as a location with higher opposition to rights for gay and lesbian people.

The South provides fertile ground for studying Christianity and gay and lesbian civil rights. The South, and Mississippi in particular, is an exemplary location to conduct a study about the interactions of Christianity and support for gay and lesbian rights because of the higher rate of religious and political conservatism (Pew Forum 2014) and the state's lack of supportive policies and legal protections for the gay and lesbian community. Located in the Deep South and the heart of the Bible Belt, Mississippi continues to be one of the most religiously and politically conservative states in the nation. According to the Pew Forum (2014), while only about 25 percent of those who identify as Christian in the United States identify as evangelical Protestant, in the South that number is 34 percent. In Mississippi, the percentage of evangelical Protestants rises to 41 percent (Pew Forum 2014). In contrast, Catholics constitute around 20 percent of Christians in the United States, while only 4 percent of Mississippians identify as Catholic (Pew Forum 2014).[6]

In addition to the conservative religious nature of the South, and largely due to this conservatism, the South is also a place of conservative political beliefs where gay and lesbian experiences are marginalized. This should not be surprising, considering that white evangelicals' support of same-sex marriage remains the lowest of all religious traditions. Only 35 percent of evangelical Protestants support same-sex marriage today, compared to 67 percent of Catholics and 68 percent of mainline Protestants (Pew Forum 2017). Although the state must adhere to changing federal legislation in regards to gay and lesbian equality, the backlash against the expanding rights of gay and lesbian citizens and reactive policies in the state, such as "religious freedom" bills,[7] make the relationship between religion and prejudice extremely clear. Specifically, these reactive laws and policies indicate that many Christians place their conservative religious beliefs above their relationships with gay and lesbian friends and family members.

One recent example of this backlash in Mississippi was House Bill 1523 (HB 1523), which Governor Phil Bryant signed on April 5, 2016. This legislation legalized discrimination in the state of Mississippi. House Bill 1523 ensured that state government would *not* punish individuals who refused to serve others on the basis of religious opposition to same-sex marriage, extramarital sex, or transgender identities. In Bryant's own words, HB 1523 was "to protect sincerely held religious beliefs and moral convictions . . . from discriminatory action by state government" (Domonoske 2016). Bryant argued this bill does not limit the rights of any citizens, but rather merely reinforces the right to religious freedom. In essence, under the protection of law, Mississippians were provided the ability to deny services to LGBTQ individuals if their "lifestyles"[8] violate the beliefs and convictions of a religious group (Tan 2016). Despite attempts to stop the legislation from taking effect, the bill became law on October 10, 2017.

Despite the religious and political conservatism of Mississippi, it is still home to many gay and lesbian people. One issue with framing the South, and specifically Mississippi, as a single-minded location where conservative Christianity reigns and gay and lesbian rights are a nonissue is that this view ignores the South as a location for the struggle for gay and lesbian equality. In fact, much of the invisibility of LGBTQ issues in the South is a direct result of the one-sided portrayal of the region.

Recent events in Mississippi show this caricature of the South is not the full story. The Human Rights Campaign (HRC) opened a state office in Mississippi in 2014 to advocate for gay and lesbian equality across the state. The presence of the HRC in a Southern state indicates a move toward queer visibility in the South. On October 20, 2014, two same-sex couples filed the first federal challenge to the same-sex marriage ban in Mississippi. In the case, *Campaign for Southern Equality v. Bryant*, the district court judge ruled that denying same-sex couples the right to marry was unconstitutional (Freedom to Marry 2018a). To date, there are no nondiscrimination laws that protect LGBTQ people across the state of Mississippi, but some cities have begun to pass such legislation, including Jackson, the state's capital, in July 2016.

The combination of conservative religion and the move toward gay and lesbian rights within the state of Mississippi make it an excellent context to explore the importance of having gay or lesbian friends or family in lending support for LGBTQ rights. The high correlation between evangelical Christianity and prejudice toward gay and lesbian people makes Mississippi a key battleground state for gay and lesbian civil rights. As Mississippi continues to move toward equality for gay and lesbian citizens, it is important to understand the barriers to gaining full equality.

Through this research, I provide a starting point for understanding the relationship between Christianity and sexuality in the South. This project answers the call for more qualitative research on the topic of Christianity and sexuality "in order to flesh out more fully the explanations provided by men and women for their opinions towards various same-sex practices" and rights (Perry and Whitehead 2016). In order to more fully understand Christians' beliefs and attitudes toward homosexuality and gay and lesbian rights, readers must attempt to suspend judgments against gay and lesbian people or conservative Christians and to truly listen to what the interviewees in this study had to say. I begin by asking the basic questions to which our society typically assumes the answers: What do Mississippi Christians believe about homosexuality, and how do these beliefs vary based on religious affiliation? What do Mississippi Christians believe about gay and lesbian civil rights, and how do these beliefs vary based on religious affiliation? What influence does having a gay or lesbian friend or family member have on these beliefs and attitudes toward homosexuality and civil rights? How do Christians reconcile their religious beliefs with their personal relationships with gay and lesbian individuals?

And finally, how does this reconciliation vary based on religious affiliation?

This study advances our understanding of how having a friend or relative who identifies as gay or lesbian influences Christians' beliefs and attitudes toward homosexuality and civil rights. I provided interview respondents many opportunities to explain the nuanced reasons having a friend or family member who is gay or lesbian influences, or does not influence, their beliefs and attitudes toward homosexuality and gay and lesbian rights. Before discussing respondents' beliefs and attitudes, I discuss my standpoint on this issue in order to answer the question Regina posed at the beginning of this chapter about my ability to be objective in this project.

Who Am I? My Unique Standpoint

Growing up in a Christian home as a lesbian in the rural South, I understand the tension between the desire to be one's authentic self and the fear of coming out and being ostracized or worse. It is from this place of personal understanding that I approach this topic. For decades, feminist scholars have stressed the importance of how a person's standpoint influences their view of the world and how individuals' unique locations make complete objectivity an unreachable goal (Collins 1986; Haraway 1988; Smith 1987). As a researcher, it is my duty to acknowledge my particular viewpoint while simultaneously appreciating and highlighting the viewpoints of those who participated in this study (Smith 1987; Zuberi and Bonilla-Silva 2008). Because every person holds a unique perspective on the world and sees the world from a particular vantage point, the more perspectives we have on a subject, the more understanding we can gain. I do not claim to have all the knowledge in this field based on my own experience or my research, but my experience coupled with others' experiences can help us to begin to understand the complex relationship between Christianity and sexuality. By understanding my position and my struggles, the reader can gain a more complete understanding of the story this research tells.

I was born and raised in a rural town in South Carolina. I was baptized in a small United Methodist church as an infant and raised in that church until I left for college at eighteen. Although my family attended a mainline denomination, being in a small town in South Carolina meant that religious and political conservatism ran through the majority of churches despite denominational teachings. In addition to my religious background, my worldview is also greatly influenced by growing up with a single mom in a white, working-class family.

After leaving my small town for college, I finally allowed myself to realize that I identify as a lesbian, and thus began the never-ending coming out process. Coming out as a lesbian led me to ask a number of questions: How could the church, which had such an important impact on my life, be a central source of my oppression and self-questioning? How could the people who watched me grow up now judge me based on my sexuality? Would knowing someone personally who identifies as gay or lesbian change their beliefs, or would they no longer see the person they helped raise but rather only my sexuality? As a lesbian raised in the Deep South, I questioned why it is that many Christians are so opposed to homosexuality. I questioned why people understood homosexuality to be such an abomination yet ignored numerous other Old Testament teachings such as prohibitions against eating shrimp (Leviticus 11:9–12), wearing clothing made of mixed fabrics (Leviticus 19:19), and commands to feed the poor (Isaiah 58:10–11).

This is where this project began—out of my personal desire to understand how a religion I was taught was based on tolerance, love, and forgiveness could breed so much fear and prejudice. It began out of my need to understand how friends and families could ostracize someone close to them because of who that person loves. This questioning and searching for answers ultimately led me to distance myself from Christianity. While I still find spirituality to be an important part of my life, I no longer identify with the Christian faith in which I was raised. It took separating myself from this faith and belief system for me to be able to accept myself for who I am: a lesbian genderqueer person living in the Southeast who was able to marry their partner because of the fight for gay and lesbian civil rights. This is my unique standpoint for understanding the topic of Christianity and sexuality.

So to respond to Regina's concern ("You're gay, right? I'll do the interview if you think you can be objective"): although my struggle with my own sexuality and religion has shaped my questions, I have strived throughout this project to be as balanced and as fair as possible to my respondents. From my subjective location, I offer in this book a glance at the inner thoughts of Christians who can at times use their own religion to turn away those they love. As difficult as this project was to complete, I now believe I have a greater understanding of why some Christians are opposed to homosexuality and why they feel it is best to terminate relationships if they cannot encourage gay and lesbian people to change their sexuality. My hope is that this study may help the reader gain some insight about Christians who cannot accept their own friends' and family members' sexuality and relationships. While this project has expanded my understanding of some Christians' opposition to homosexuality, it is in no way my intention to stand up for this viewpoint or to justify it. Although I may better understand the reasoning of some conservative Christians, I cannot accept a religious tradition that leads to the pain and suffering of others. As Barton (2012) explains in *Pray the Gay Away: The Extraordinary Lives of Bible Belt Gays*, "Because most Christian churches in the Bible Belt construct homosexuality as sinful, lesbians and gay men from the region must choose between staying in . . . the 'toxic closet' or risk rejection and ostracism from the people who are supposed to care for them most—their families, friends, and neighbors" (4–5). Supporting conservative Christians' opposition to homosexuality and gay and lesbian rights is dangerous to the lives of gay and lesbian people and especially to gay and lesbian youth who must choose between the "toxic closet" and risking everything.

I hope this account of who I am and why this topic is important to me demonstrates that my approach can never be completely objective and yet strives to be balanced. As Bartkowski (2004) explains, it is impossible for social scientists to "treat their subject matter like an 'object'" (18), but I do strive to provide a balanced consideration of the subject. I attempt to balance an empathetic understanding of Mississippi Christians' beliefs and attitudes toward gay and lesbian people, while simultaneously organizing them into a broader picture of the changing relationship between Christianity and homosexuality in the South.

Book Overview

In this book, I draw from interviews with Mississippi Christians to examine beliefs and attitudes toward homosexuality and gay and lesbian civil rights and to explore how knowing someone who identifies as gay or lesbian influences these beliefs and attitudes. In chapters 1 and 2, I provide an overview of respondents' beliefs about Christianity, the Bible, and their beliefs and attitudes toward homosexuality. The issue of homosexuality has been a hot-button issue among Christians for some time. From James Dobson's (evangelical Christian and founder of Focus on the Family) loud and clear condemnation of homosexuality, to Gene Robinson's election as the first openly gay bishop of the Episcopalian church in 2003, to the United Methodist Church's continuing debate over ordaining gay and lesbian pastors, the issue of homosexuality continues to be controversial for Christians in the United States. The respondents in this study fall along this continuum, which ranges from complete opposition to full acceptance of gay and lesbian people. In chapters 3, 4, and 5, I discuss the respondents' views about gay and lesbian civil rights and examine the nuances within these beliefs. Although Southerners have been painted with a single brushstroke as politically and religiously conservative, in reality they demonstrate varying degrees of support and opposition to gay and lesbian rights. Specifically, chapter 3 considers the right of same-sex marriage[9]; chapter 4, same-sex adoption; and chapter 5, the respondents' beliefs and attitudes about the gay and lesbian civil rights. In chapter 6, I examine how respondents' beliefs and attitudes about homosexuality and gay and lesbian civil rights are influenced by relationships with individuals who identify as gay or lesbian. Finally, I conclude with a look at the current political climate in the United States with regards to gay and lesbian rights, and I offer recommendations for scholars and activists working with gay and lesbian people.

My goal is to provide a deeper understanding of how Christians make sense of their relationships with gay and lesbian people while simultaneously practicing a religion often interpreted to condemn homosexuality. Research indicates that having friends and family members from a group different from your own should lead to more positive beliefs and attitudes toward the members of that group (Allport 1954), yet conservative Christians continue to hold increased negative beliefs and attitudes toward gay and lesbian people. Therefore, I examine whether having a relationship with a gay or lesbian person is *enough* to overcome negative beliefs and attitudes about homosexuality and lead to more support of gay and lesbian civil rights.

PART 1

Religion and Homosexuality

1

God Said Love Thy Neighbor, Unless They're Gay

[Conversation with interviewee at the completion of a phone interview]

ANGELA (fifty-three-year-old, white evangelical Protestant from the Gulf Coast): Are you a Christian?

ME: I grew up in the United Methodist Church, but I do not identify as Christian now.

ANGELA: I'm confused. Did you grow up knowing the love of Jesus Christ?

ME: I grew up in the church being taught about Jesus.

ANGELA: Then why are you not Christian?

ME: I believe in some higher power but do not believe that Jesus is the only path to god.

ANGELA: Then what God do you believe in?

ME: I believe in the same god as you. I believe that all religions that teach love, acceptance, and compassion worship the same god and that Jesus is not the only one path to god.

ANGELA: Then I guess you have not read the Bible.

ME: Actually, I have read the Bible.

ANGELA: I'm confused. How is that possible? I knew another person who grew up in the church, even sang in the gospel choir, who turned their back on God. I do not understand this. I guess that's a lot of Satan's doing. I will be praying for you. Are you a homosexual?

ME: I identify as a lesbian.

ANGELA: Again, I will be praying for you, I would hate for the end of the world to come and for you to be left behind.

ME: Thank you. If that is what you feel like you need to do, I respect that.

While my personal ties to this research allowed me to more thoroughly understand the topic and to ask better questions, my insider position also made the research process extremely stressful. As the conversation at the beginning of this chapter indicates, many of the interviews were difficult to sit through. From the assumptions of interviewees about my beliefs and sexual orientation to the continuous attempts to devalue the lives of gay and lesbian people—including my own life—because of our sexuality, I found this project to be simultaneously rewarding and emotionally draining. As Erzen (2006) explained, once qualitative researchers begin to study groups they disagree with, they have to "grapple with conflicting emotions and expectations when the social and religious conservatism of the people or groups they study reflect moral and political ideals that are distinct from their own" (7). She continued by explaining how these studies of conservative groups in the United States "highlight crucial questions about what it means to have a fieldwork agenda when one's research subjects are conservative Christians with their own conversionary agendas for the researcher" (7). As the conversation with Angela at the beginning of this chapter highlighted, some of the evangelical Protestant interviewees indeed had their own agenda in mind when agreeing to participate in this study. They used this opportunity to evangelize—try to convert me to Christianity, specifically their version of Christianity. In addition to Angela, nine other evangelical Protestants from Mississippi agreed to be interviewed for this study.[1]

In contrast to the evangelical Protestant interviewees, and despite living in the Deep South, many Mississippi Christians were very supportive of gay and lesbian people. They spoke of Christianity's mandate to love one's neighbor and spoke of a God who was nonjudgmental. A growing portion of Mississippians, specifically mainline Protestants and more liberal Catholics, wished to open church doors to gay and lesbian congregants and leave the judging to their God. About half (nineteen out of forty) of the Mississippi Christians who agreed to participate in an interview identified as mainline Protestants.[2]

Mainline Protestants' more liberal theology and beliefs about homosexuality fit more closely with secular society's growing acceptance of gay and lesbian rights. In fact, these beliefs could be part of the reason for stagnation in mainline Protestantism. Smith et al. (1998) reveal how evangelicals' embattled status with society enables them to continue to thrive, while mainline Protestantism is on the decline. According to Smith et al. (1998), evangelical Protestants thrive because of the boundaries and distinctions they create between themselves and secular society. Mainline Protestants do not attempt to set themselves apart from society in the same way; rather, they engage with society and are more open to differences in beliefs and ideology. Smith et al. (1998) suggest that by not distinguishing themselves from the larger society, mainline Protestants lose their distinctiveness, which leads to decline. A recent study conducted by the Pew Forum (2015) found that mainline Protestants declined by 3.4 percent as a share of the U.S. population between 2007 and 2014. During this same period, evangelical Protestants declined less than 1 percent.

Eleven out of the forty respondents attended a Catholic church.[3] Catholics' beliefs and attitudes fell between those of evangelical and mainline Protestants on many issues. This makes sense because unlike Protestants, who divide into different denominations based on specific theological and social beliefs, Catholics pride themselves on remaining one officially united church (Konieczny 2013; Manning 1999). This means when differences in beliefs occur, Catholics do not splinter off into separate churches in the same way Protestants might. Granted, in more highly populous Catholic regions of the country, some parishes develop reputations for being more conservative or liberal, which may attract specific Catholics. However, in Mississippi and other areas of the country that are not heavily Catholic, the inclusion of conservative and liberal Catholics in a single parish is more common. Clearly this leads to a wider range of beliefs and opinions within Catholic churches in the region, as both liberal and conservative Catholics work side by side within the same church organizations (Manning 1999).

As previously mentioned, most Catholics in the United States today no longer feel that it is necessary to rely on the Vatican's teaching authority. In fact, D'Antonio et al. (2013) found that only 35 percent of Catholics indicated the church's opposition to same-sex marriage was very important to them. (It is important to remember that D'Antonio et al.'s data were collected before the election of Pope Francis in 2013.) This minimization of distinctiveness could explain why the Catholic population in the United States is declining at a similar rate to mainline Protestants. Between 2007 and 2014, the proportion of Catholics in the United States declined by 3.1 percent (Pew Forum 2015).

Religious Beliefs and Prejudice

Though different denominations interpret the Bible differently, each denomination strives to uphold what they believe the Bible mandates. It is also true that the more conservative the denomination's approach to understanding the Bible—that is, the more literally they interpret the text—the less likely they are to accept anything that contradicts their understanding of their religion. Thus the more members of a denomination believe their religion holds absolute truths, the less likely they are to change their positions on issues.

Specifically related to the issue of homosexuality, the more a person believes that their religion holds absolute truths, the more likely they are to hold negative views toward gay and lesbian people (Rowatt et al. 2006). Research has demonstrated that of those who identify as Christian, evangelical Protestants are most likely to condemn homosexuality and express prejudice toward gay and lesbian people (Duck and Hunsberger 1999; Hill et al. 2010) and are least likely to support gay and lesbian rights (Sherkat et al. 2011). Overall, people who belong to conservative religious groups hold more traditional religious views, attend church more often, and have a greater likelihood of holding negative beliefs and attitudes toward gay and lesbian individuals (Hinrichs and Rosenberg 2002).

The link between religion and prejudice is not only based on specific religious beliefs but also linked to a person's overall worldview and fear. Research points to three important aspects that influence an individual's prejudice toward gay and lesbian people: first, a person's overall belief systems; second, a person's specific beliefs about the origins of an individual's homosexuality (as a choice, a biological trait, or caused by the social environment); and finally, a person's perception of a threat to their beliefs or worldview (Baker and Brauner-Otto 2015; Hill et al. 2010; McVeigh and Diaz 2009; Whitley 2009; Wilkinson 2004). Since many religions condemn homosexuality, individuals within these belief systems often internalize these negative views toward gay and lesbian people (Hill et al. 2010). Because some Christians' overall belief system indicates homosexuality is sinful, these individuals translate these beliefs into action—prejudice and discrimination—against gay and lesbian people. If a Christian interprets the Bible to prohibit same-sex sexual activity, as many do, and labels this behavior as sinful, then this overall belief system will be translated into how they interact with people who identify as gay or lesbian. Christians who interpret the Bible in this way often demonstrate prejudice toward gay and lesbian people because they believe gay and lesbian people are knowingly sinning and defying God's will.

David, a sixty-one-year-old white evangelical Protestant from the Mississippi Gulf Coast, demonstrated extremely prejudicial views toward gay and lesbian people during his interview. His responses clearly showed how his religious beliefs have influenced his overall belief system. David believed the Bible clearly prohibits homosexuality and that gay and lesbian people are knowingly defying the word of God. When I asked David how homosexuality should be handled within the church, he stated, "Just as I would [handle] adultery or any other sins in the Bible, because it's not any worse, it's not any better. God considers sin, sin. And what we consider small sins or large sins—God says if you violate any part of the law . . . then you've sinned. And if you sin, unless you've found grace through Jesus, you end up not where you'd like to be when it's all over with." Clearly David held a very black-and-white understanding of what the Bible teaches. The Bible says homosexuality is against Christian law, and so Christians must do everything they can to deter this behavior. According to David, it is his Christian duty to make sure that gay and lesbian people do not go to hell. David felt justified in his condemnation of homosexuality and in denying rights to those who defy the will of God, because in his mind, he was trying to help them.

The second important mechanism of prejudice toward gay and lesbian people is a person's belief about the nature of homosexuality. Whether someone believes that being gay or lesbian is a choice, a biological trait, or caused by the social environment has a tremendous influence on prejudice toward gay and lesbian people (Baker and Brauner-Otto 2015; Whitley 2009). The belief that people choose their sexuality, a belief promoted by some Christian churches, is strongly connected with antigay beliefs and attitudes. If a person believes a behavior perceived to be deviant can be controlled, they generally hold more negative attitudes toward people who engage in that behavior (Whitley 2009). Take, for example, alcoholism, which some respondents in this study compared to homosexuality. Many conservative Christians believe that drinking alcohol is sinful and that alcoholics can choose not to engage in this behavior. Accordingly, levels of prejudice against this group increase because the behavior is perceived to be controllable.

For instance, one evangelical Protestant, Candace, a sixty-year-old white woman from the Mississippi Gulf Coast, explained that she believes homosexuality is a choice and everyone is prone to certain weaknesses. Because homosexuality is viewed as a choice in her perspective, she argued that gay and lesbian people can and should attempt to change their sexuality. She continued by comparing homosexuality to drug and alcohol addiction:

It would take the person desiring to be free . . . because I think there's spiritual stuff going on there and it's like a drug addict. Can a heroin addict be free? And I do think the answer is yes. Is it easy? No. And so, can an alcoholic be free? Yes. Is it easy? No. Because their mind is constantly wanting to draw them back to what they knew. . . . You know, some people are set free like this; God just sovereignly moves and takes that desire away. Some people have to constantly walk putting God first in their lives every moment, every step of the way, and asking him for strength and help to walk in a way that is pleasing to him.

Because Candace believed that homosexuality is something a person chooses, or at the least something they struggle with because of family situations, she believed gay and lesbian people must attempt to overcome this "sin."

Lastly, if Christians perceive gay and lesbian people to be a threat to American or religious values—as many evangelical Protestants and conservative Catholics do—this perceived threat increases negative attitudes (McVeigh and Diaz 2009). For example, many conservative Christians view same-sex marriage as a threat to their religious beliefs concerning the meaning of marriage. Conservative Catholics, specifically those who continue to uphold the authority of the church on social issues, view those acting on same-sex desires to be in conflict with the church's teachings, as the Vatican has historically been completely opposed to homosexuality. Acceptance of homosexuality is viewed as a threat to the foundation of the Catholic faith and the teachings of the church. For instance, as of 2011, the majority (52 percent) of Catholics continued to agree with the church's opposition to same-sex marriage (D'Antonio et al. 2013).

Many people also feel same-sex marriage is a threat to American values, specifically what is often referred to as the "traditional" family. Based on the view that men and women complement or even complete one another in marriage, conservative Christians often feel as if marriage between two partners of the same sex threatens the entire foundation of society, which they argue is the nuclear family. Seeing gay and lesbian people as a threat to American and religious values greatly increases negative beliefs and attitudes toward this population.

Andrew, a middle-aged white pastor at an evangelical Protestant church along the Gulf Coast of Mississippi, is one of the interviewees who expressed this sentiment succinctly. When I asked Andrew if gay and lesbian people should be allowed to legally marry, he explained that although homosexuality had existed forever, this did not mean that we should now begin to call it marriage: "I think that when we redefine terms of basic societal relationships, I think that you're losing the foundation for society." He went on to explain that calling same-sex unions marriage undermines our entire basis of community. Andrew felt that using the label "marriage" was a threat to his religious beliefs and to America's societal values.

Subcultural Identity among Mississippi Christians

So why do some Christians, especially evangelical Protestants and conservative Catholics, continue to hold prejudicial views against homosexuality and gay and lesbian civil rights? Is this merely an issue of biblical interpretation? How do Christianity and the Bible lead different respondents to such varied beliefs about what is right or wrong? One important element to answering these questions is subcultural identity. Based on feelings of similarity and likeness, individuals develop a sense of membership in groups (Hogg and Abrams 1988). In order for groups to form, there must be some "other"—there must be other groups to whom people *do not* belong (Hogg and Abrams 1988). Theories of group identity suggest that through the process of forming groups, members often develop negative attitudes and stereotypes about those who do not fit into their own group. Additionally, individuals develop identities and a sense of self based on their group memberships (Hogg, Terry, and White 1995; Stets and Burke 2000). Therefore, the stronger and more closed-off the boundaries around a group, the stronger the group will become. Weak or open group boundaries suggest anyone can come into or leave a group at any time. Groups with weak or open boundaries do not foster the same degree of commitment and buy-in as groups with stronger boundaries. Strong or closed boundaries make it easier for group members to compare themselves to the "other." This leads to a higher degree of commitment to the group and a stronger sense of identity based on group membership.

Originally, Smith et al. (1998) used subcultural identity theory to demonstrate how evangelical Protestants used religion as a primary mechanism to form their social identity. Through this theory, the authors show that evangelical Protestants rely heavily on social comparisons between themselves and others for the construction of their identity. According to subcultural identity theory, evangelical Protestants develop a more salient religious identity and thrive as a religious tradition *because* they distinguish themselves from others (Smith et al. 1998). While mainline Protestants and Catholics also compare themselves to other groups, Smith et al. (1998) show that evangelical Protestants stressed distinction far more than other Christian traditions.

For example, when I asked Erica, a sixty-three-year-old white evangelical Protestant from the Gulf Coast, her opinion of other churches who do not agree that homosexuality is always sinful, she explained, "I think [the other churches] are deceived. I think that it's not the full word of God, if you just pick and choose what parts of the Bible you accept." She clearly separated her faith in God and understanding of the Bible from other Christians who disagreed with her interpretation. Erica established the importance of sexuality as a boundary around evangelical Protestantism. This evangelical Protestant boundary is built and supported by the Bible and moral accountability. As Manning (1999) explains, evangelical Protestants' "emphasis on moral accountability reflects a characteristically Protestant emphasis on moralism: the designation of a strict code [outlined in the Bible] combined with the expectation that anyone who violates the code deserves to be punished" (219). Violating the Bible is dangerous not only for those breaking the code but also for the world. The evangelical Protestants in this study clearly demonstrate their fear that gay and lesbian people will be punished for breaking the code of moral accountability and that the nation and world will also suffer for their failings.

Understanding theories of identity is important when considering Christians' beliefs and attitudes toward gay and lesbian people, because gay and lesbian people constitute a group that conservative Christians set themselves apart from in order to create their Christian identity. In fact, evangelicalism "is strong not because it's shielded against, but because it's—or at least perceives itself to be—embattled with forces that seem to oppose or threaten it" (Smith et al. 1998, 89). Gay and lesbian rights are one of many "forces" that evangelical Protestants believe they must fight. As Smith et al. (1998) show, American evangelicalism "thrives on distinction, engagement, tension, conflict, and threat" (89). Overall, evangelical Protestants base their identity on how they differ from certain mainstream values, such as support for same-sex marriage and adoption.

While subcultural identity theory was created to explain the strength of evangelical Protestantism, I expand the theory in this book in two ways. First, I examine how different religious traditions distinguish themselves to different degrees and in distinctive ways from mainstream society. I also add mainline Protestants and Catholics to this continuum of distinction. Second, I expand subcultural identity theory by more thoroughly defining the cultural mainstream. The idea of a mainstream culture in this theory has been largely undertheorized, as the theory assumes there exists a single, coherent mainstream. Consequently, it is necessary to discuss what is meant by mainstream and how this may differ based on geographic location.

In this study, each religious group varies in the type of boundaries and the degree of strength and openness of those boundaries. Overall, evangelical Protestants form a strong and closed boundary based on their literal interpretation of the Bible. Evangelical Protestants use the Bible to set themselves apart from mainstream society, and they believe that individuals must hold certain beliefs and adhere to specific practices to be a part of their group. Conservative Catholics also form a boundary around their religious tradition, but rather than this boundary being based on the literal interpretation of the Bible, it is grounded in their strict adherence to the teachings of the Catholic Church and priestly instruction. While this boundary is closed, meaning that conservative Catholics believe all Catholics must obey the teachings of the church to be a part of the group, it does not appear to keep out mainstream culture as effectively as the Bible does for evangelical Protestants. Finally, mainline Protestants and more liberal Catholics—those Catholics who do not feel they must follow the authority of the church on all issues—seem to have a lack of boundaries (or at most, highly permeable boundaries) around their religious traditions. Oftentimes mainline Protestants' and liberal Catholics' beliefs regarding social issues are one and the same with the cultural mainstream. The openness or lack of these boundaries means that there is no "other" to compare themselves to in order to build a separate identity.

In opposition to evangelical Protestantism, mainline Protestantism loses a strong sense of Christian distinctiveness through accommodation to mainstream society—what Smith et al. (1998) refer to as "engagement-without-distinction." In fact, mainline Protestants are not actually subcultural at all according to this theory. While mainline Protestants do engage with mainstream culture, and they may hold negative opinions about some conservative Christians beliefs, overall this religious tradition does not distinguish itself from the American cultural mainstream. On a continuum of distinction from the American cultural mainstream, evangelical Protestants would fall on the far end of distinction and mainline Protestants on the far end of accommodation or agreement.

This accommodation or agreement was evident in Nancy's, a fifty-year-old white mainline Protestant in northeast Mississippi, explanation of her thoughts about churches that take a stance against homosexuality. She said, "I think it's just ignorance on their part, and not really understanding human beings, and not wanting to. . . . You know, it's their loss. . . . They could have met the best person. . . . I think it's just kind of narrow-minded." Comparably, Casey, a thirty-nine-year-old white mainline Protestant living in northeast Mississippi, stated, "I don't attend those churches. They believe what they believe; I believe what I believe. I hope that anybody who feels persecuted or unhappy would look for a place that would love them as a person and could find a church that loves them as a person. . . . I feel like [churches that stand against homosexuality] are wrong, but that's their place and they're entitled to it." While mainline Protestants distinguished themselves from conservative Christians, these differences show that mainline Protestants' beliefs are more aligned with a cultural mainstream in the United States that is moving toward gay and lesbian equality. Also, Nancy's and Casey's responses demonstrated a belief that everyone has the right to believe what they want. This entitlement to different beliefs shows that mainline Protestants in this study did not feel the need to defend themselves or fight against evangelical Protestantism on the issues of homosexuality and gay and lesbian rights; that is, they did not feel embattled by the group that disagreed with them.

As previously discussed, liberal and conservative Catholics attend church alongside one another—particularly in regions of the country with a lower density of Catholics—because, unlike Protestantism, Catholicism remains united, at least in denomination. The smaller number of Catholics in the southeastern United States makes it difficult to form multiple parishes in rural areas and small cities. Despite the seeming united front, Konieczny (2013) found extreme polarization on social issues among Catholics—"even in a church that has historically tolerated pluralism and where the impulse is to remain unified rather than to separate" (9). The distinctions between conservative and liberal Catholics were evident in this study when it came to the social issue of gay and lesbian civil rights. Conservative Catholics distinguished themselves from more liberal Christians through their perceived adherence to the teachings of the Catholic Church and their priests' instructions. The issues of homosexuality and gay and lesbian rights aligned conservative Catholic politics more closely with those of evangelical Protestants. On the other hand, more liberal Catholics appeared to face the same dilemma as mainline Protestants—that is, through accommodation to American mainstream society, they lost a sense of distinctiveness.

While evangelical Protestants create an ideal subcultural identity through the use of the Bible for distinction-with-engagement, conservative Catholics distinguish themselves from the cultural mainstream through adherence to the teachings of the Catholic Church. Specifically, conservative Catholics find that "the problem with homosexuality is that it's unnatural" (Manning 1999, 207). That is, they base their opposition to homosexuality and gay and lesbian rights more on natural law theology than on the Bible. Natural law theology states that "God's will is revealed not only in the Bible (as many conservative Protestants insist) but can also be discerned by human reason through the observation of nature. . . . Because God created nature, our physical body and its natural inclinations reveal God's will" (Manning 1999, 220). According to this belief, one of those natural inclinations is "procreation and training of offspring" (Manning 1999, 220). Therefore, conservative Catholics are more likely to view gay and lesbian people as suffering from psychological issues rather than as lacking morality, as evangelical Protestants would argue (Manning 1999, 207). Based on this belief, discrimination through law will not solve the problem, and consequently, conservative Catholics are more likely to conditionally accept gay and lesbian people and rights than their conservative Protestant counterparts (Manning 1999). This does not mean that conservative Catholics accept homosexuality; in fact, most believe that gay and lesbian people should choose not to engage in same-sex relationships and should remain celibate (Manning 1999). However, they do not believe that gay and lesbian people are immoral or embattled with this "sinful" force in the way evangelical Protestants do.

Both groups of conservative Christians—evangelical Protestants and conservative Catholics—seem to be committed to reinforcing and creating new boundaries of distinction based on the Bible or the church's moral authority, respectively, when their boundaries are threatened by changing societal views. However, the Catholics in this study seemed to be only semisubcultural compared to evangelical Protestants, thereby only gaining some of the benefits of subcultural identity. Natural law theology, along with not gaining full benefits of holding a subcultural identity, is likely why conservative Catholics' responses to homosexuality and gay and lesbian rights appeared to be more ambivalent and compromising than those of evangelical Protestants.

Now, what is this amorphous "cultural mainstream" from which subcultural identity theorists suppose evangelical Protestants are setting themselves apart? Subcultural identity theory depends on there being a cultural mainstream for the subculture to resist. Although the cultural mainstream is not clearly defined in Smith et al.'s (1998) theory, it appears to be demarcated by the nationwide movement toward liberalism, acceptance, and equality. Yet in the state of Mississippi, there is a powerful cultural undertow against the American mainstream. The conservative political and religious backlash against the national trend toward equality for gay and lesbian people does not appear to be as countercultural when examining the geographical location of the South, and Mississippi in particular. This Southern subcultural undertow to the American mainstream culture may in fact weaken the boundaries of conservative Christians within the state of Mississippi. While religiously conservative Mississippians are subordinated by and embattled with the national mainstream culture on the issue of gay and lesbian civil rights, they are much more dominant within the conservative Mississippi cultural mainstream. While conservative Christians' boundaries seem more flexible and open to Mississippi's cultural undertow, it appears they may in fact gain even more power from their identity, since it is bolstered by the political landscape of the state yet remains subcultural to the nation. Hence evangelical Protestants gain actual political power in the state of Mississippi while simultaneously defining themselves against the larger mainstream culture in the United States.

Historically, gender has been one of the key boundaries used to separate conservative Christians from the nationwide mainstream culture. "Traditional gender roles" and "traditional family values" are catchphrases used by Republicans and the Religious Right to reinforce how conservative Christians differ from mainstream culture, especially gay and lesbian culture. But over time, these gender boundaries have weakened due to changing economic conditions and women's equality. As these gender boundaries continue to weaken within Christianity, I contend that sexuality is being used to bolster and reinforce conservative Christians' beliefs and ideology about gender. Consequently, in order to understand the importance of conservative Christians' opposition to homosexuality and gay and lesbian rights, I must first explain the changing meaning of gender within conservative Christianity.

Reinforcing the Gender Boundary with Sexuality

Gender ideology has long been a critical boundary for conservative Christians and a major contributing factor to the condemnation of homosexuality (Gallagher 2004; Konieczny 2013). People who hold strong beliefs in "traditional" gender roles and family structures (i.e., with a man as breadwinner and a woman as homemaker) are less accepting of breaks in expected gender-specific behavior and sexual behavior (Bartkowski 2001; Baunach, Burgess, and Muse 2010; Hinrichs and Rosenberg 2002; McVeigh and Diaz 2009). As Butler (1990) explained with her concept of the "heterosexual matrix," based on a person's perceived biological sex, they are expected to perform a certain gender—masculine or feminine—and to be sexually attracted to those who perform the opposite gender. According to Butler (1990), the heterosexual matrix "designates that grid of cultural intelligibility through which bodies, gender and desires are naturalized . . . a hegemonic discursive/epistemic model of gender intelligibility that assumes that for bodies to cohere and make sense there must be a stable sex expressed through a stable gender (masculine expresses male, feminine expresses female) that is oppositional and hierarchically defined through compulsory practice of heterosexuality" (151). In other words, males should identify and act like men, which includes being attracted to women, while females should identify and act like women, which includes being attracted to men.

Evangelical Protestants and conservative Catholics hold tightly to this essentialist understanding of sex, gender, and sexuality. By stressing the importance of bodies, expressions, and desires aligning, conservative Christian communities emphasize the significance of "traditional" gender roles and family structure. Based on these beliefs, conservative Christians are generally more opposed to same-sex marriage and adoption—and gay and lesbian civil rights more broadly—than the American cultural mainstream. In general, heterosexual families who hold rigid gender expectations (e.g., that women take care of children and the home while men work outside of the home and make the money) remain the ideal within conservative Christianity (Gallagher 2004; McQueeney 2009).

EVANGELICAL PROTESTANTS: SYMBOLIC TRADITIONALISM AND PRAGMATIC EGALITARIANISM

A substantial body of research shows that evangelical Protestants consistently support more traditional gender norms than mainline Protestants or Americans more generally (Bartkowski 2001; Brasher 1998; Gallagher 2003; Gallagher and Smith 1999; Griffith 1997). In fact, evangelicals often blame various social problems in the United States and the world on weakened gender boundaries, and they promote traditional gender roles and family structures as a panacea for these problems (Bartkowski 2004; Kelly 2012; Schreiber 2008). These beliefs become evident when considering the continued ideal of wifely submission within evangelical Protestant households (Bartkowski 2001; Brasher 1998; Gallagher and Smith 1999; Griffith 1997). As Hankins (2008) explains, "The ideal undergirding the Southern Baptist [an evangelical Protestant denomination] submission statement . . . known as the complementarian view . . . [is] the idea that men and women are inherently different by nature and have different roles in families, churches, and societies" (119). In short, men and women are thought to complement one another so that after marriage, they become a single whole. Supporters of a complementarian view, typically evangelical Protestants, argue that men and women are created equal but different based on gender and that "God ordains the distinctions between the roles of men and women" (Hankins 2008, 120). This rigid gender ideology, which remains an ideal within many conservative Christian communities, excludes gay and lesbian people from the image of a healthy family (Gallagher 2003; Manning 1999). The only way for a person to become whole, according to this view, is to marry someone of the opposite sex. By marrying someone of the same sex, one role will go unfulfilled, and the family will not be healthy or as God intended.

Despite evangelical Protestants' consistent rhetoric concerning the need for "traditional" gender and family roles, their actual gender practices are far more complex than this ideology would suggest. Over the past two decades, scholars have exposed an increasingly egalitarian model of gender and family within evangelical Protestantism, even as rhetoric has remained largely constant (Bartkowski 2001; Brasher 1998; Gallagher 2003; Gallagher and Smith 1999; Griffith 1997). This shift from "pure" wifely submission and husband headship to a growing acceptance of mutual submission (Bartkowski 2001; Bartkowski and Read 2003; Brasher 1998; Griffith 1997; Manning 1999) has slowly weakened the subcultural identity boundary of gender. Even men and women who continue to rhetorically support wifely submission and husband headship typically fall short of this standard in actual practice. The growing economic necessity for women to work outside of the home and the push for men to be more involved fathers and husbands have led to remarkable changes in gender relations within the evangelical Protestant family (Bartkowski 2001, 2004). With over half of all women in today's workforce and men doing more household labor than ever before, how do evangelical Protestants continue to support their conservative views of gender and family?

Gallagher and Smith (1999) found that while the vast majority of evangelical Protestant respondents agreed with "traditional" views of gender and family, most combined egalitarian ideas—a belief in equality and equal rights of all people—with traditional ones while continuing to emphasize male headship "as a core family value" (217). Most evangelicals viewed women's employment as necessary and did not view joint decision-making as conflicting with the ideology of male headship. Many exchanged "symbolic support of male headship" for a more realistic practice of what Gallagher and Smith (1999) refer to as "mutual respect" (225). Overall, Gallagher and Smith (1999) concluded that symbolic traditionalism (a belief in the value of the "traditional" family model) and pragmatic egalitarianism (dividing family roles more equally among men and women in heterosexual families) best described how both men and women have internalized traditional values that are increasingly difficult to obtain. The continuance of symbolic ideals enables men to deal with the loss of ability to be the primary breadwinner and women to feel like "good wives." On the other hand, pragmatic egalitarianism enables the family to function within a changing society that encourages women to join the formal workforce and generally necessitates it for financial reasons.

As American society continues to move toward gender equality, evangelical Protestants hold onto the ideals of male headship and wifely submission as boundary markers from society at large. Their strong stance against feminist efforts to bring about gender equality in society (Manning 1999; Schreiber 2008) and maintenance of traditional gender ideologies (Gallagher and Smith 1999) indicate that gender is a symbol for something deeper and more important than a surface level analysis would suggest. The complexity of the issue of gender for evangelical Protestants necessitates a more clear-cut boundary to ensure their embattled status in a national mainstream culture that continues to move toward equality. Consequently, while evangelicals practice a pragmatic egalitarianism when it comes to gender, this egalitarianism is not replicated when it comes to gay and lesbian people. Evangelicals, by and large, are less likely to bend to cultural forces when it comes to the issue of sexuality. This allows them to survive in a society that requires women to work outside the home while also allowing them to maintain a firm boundary from the national mainstream culture.

Conservative Catholics, who continue to largely oppose same-sex marriage, base their views largely on the historical teachings of the Catholic Church. Yet while conservative Catholics condemn homosexuality, like evangelical Protestants "they have a very different view of what causes these problems and how they should be solved"(Manning 1999, 204). As Konieczny (2013) explains, conservative Catholics continue to follow the church's conviction that sex and intimacy should only occur within marriage for the purpose of procreation. Therefore, homosexuality is "wrong because [it] prevents reproduction, the natural outcome of sex" (Manning 1999, 221)—not because gay and lesbian people are immoral or devastating to society. In addition, similar to an evangelical perspective, contemporary marriage within Catholicism is based in Catholics' understanding of "how particular gender roles and relations in marriage have been religiously supported historically" (Konieczny 2013, 105). Just as there is a divide between evangelical and mainline Protestants over the issue of marriage and family, Konieczny (2013) finds a similar division between conservative and liberal Catholics. His research demonstrates that in a more conservative Catholic church, authority relations to the church and beliefs about gender roles are intertwined with the church's teachings about contraception; together, Konieczny shows that these factors influence how families are formed and what constitutes family. On the other hand, at a more liberal Catholic church, the emphasis was on egalitarian family relations, and the members had various responses to the authority of church teachings, specifically when it came to marriage and family.

Manning (1999) explains that the Catholic Church's relationship to American culture and gender and family norms is different than that of Protestants. Due to Catholics' historic immigrant- and working-class status in the United States, they did not acquire the same privileges as white Protestants. Consequently, in early Catholic history in the United States, women within the religion found it hard, if not impossible, "to meet the standards of Victorian womanhood" (Manning 1999, 229). That is, many Catholic women were forced to work outside of the home at an earlier time than white Protestants and, because of this, had to reconsider the "natural" role of women in society sooner. Manning (1999) argues that while Catholic women held on to "traditional gender norms longer than Protestants . . . they did not develop the kind of coherent antifeminist ideology that emerged among conservative Protestants. Their response to early twentieth-century feminism was ambiguous" (230). In this study, I show that conservative Catholics in Mississippi have a similarly ambiguous response to gay and lesbian rights in our society today.

At the time of this study, the Catholic Church still took an official stance against homosexuality, even as some individual Catholics' attitudes had shifted with society in general toward equality. For example, D'Antonio et al. (2013) found that in 1987, only 20 percent of pre–Vatican II Catholics (born in 1940 or earlier) surveyed indicated the moral authority on homosexual behavior should rest with the individual. By 2011, fully half of pre–Vatican II Catholics believed moral authority on homosexual behavior was fully an individuals' decision. Additionally, D'Antonio et al. (2013) found that Catholics were more likely than other religiously affiliated Americans to support same-sex marriage.

Yet while conservative Catholics overall remain opposed to homosexuality, "they are aware that many other [people] in their church support tolerance for gays and lesbians . . . [and they] do not want their opposition to homosexuality to be labeled as intolerant and reactionary" (Manning 1999, 207). Hence when it comes to rights for gay and lesbian people, conservative Catholics appear to be more accepting than evangelical Protestants. While it is a conditional acceptance of gay and lesbian rights, it does blur the boundaries and make conservative Catholics only semisubcultural when compared to evangelical Protestants. Conservative Catholics use beliefs about homosexuality and gay and lesbian rights to set themselves apart from more liberal Catholics, but to a lesser degree from mainstream culture. As Manning (1999) explains, conservative Catholics' "most immediate struggle is not with the secular society but with liberal Catholics" (207). Since Pope Francis publicly spoke out about being more accepting of gay and lesbian people, there may have been some confusion among participants on what the Catholic Church's official position is on the issue of homosexuality. Nevertheless, when I collected the data for this project in 2013, the church's stance was still presumed to be that homosexuality was sinful, and Catholics who upheld the moral authority of church leaders would be opposed to gay and lesbian rights. Based on this understanding, many of the Catholics in this study opposed homosexuality and gay and lesbian rights, but they did so more hesitantly than evangelical Protestants. This hesitance, or even conditional acceptance, was likely because conservative Catholics continued to worship and interact with more liberal Catholics in the same institutions. This led them to be more sympathetic to gay and lesbian people or at least to not want to appear cruel to fellow Catholics (Manning 1999).

* * * * *

Traditional gender, family, and sexual ideologies have historically separated conservative Christians from the broader society and from their more liberal counterparts. Nevertheless, as conservative gender and family ideologies become less and less practical, many conservative Christians are attempting to reinforce the gender boundary by shifting their focus to sexuality. Although gender and sexuality are two different components of identity, they are highly related concepts, especially within conservative Christianity. As Butler (1990) explained with her concept of the "heterosexual matrix," most people assume that all individuals are born male or female, express the gender associated with that biological sex (masculinity or femininity, respectively), and then are sexually attracted to those with the opposite biological sex and gender expression. This binary view of sex, gender, and sexuality are extremely pronounced within conservative Christianity.

As conservative Christian gender and family ideologies become less rational for today's society, these ideologies can be bolstered by an increased focus on "expected" sexuality. Using sexuality as a boundary marker between conservative Christians and mainstream society appears to be an attempt to preserve elements of "traditional" gender ideology, while simultaneously letting go of those elements that are impossible to live out today. In the midst of this weakening gender boundary marker, I contend that beliefs about homosexuality have in many ways reinforced the failing gender boundary—a trend that is most evident among evangelical Protestants. In fact, evangelical Protestants' cultural accommodation of changing gender norms is likely a chief reason for their persistent intolerance of gay and lesbian people.

By drawing a hard line against homosexuality, conservative Christians have successfully protected their subcultural identity from assimilation with the larger society. Wellman (2008) concurs that within evangelicalism, gender is being downplayed and is no longer "the burning issue"; rather, evangelical Protestants are emphasizing their opposition to same-sex marriage and the "normalization" of homosexuality as key issues in their fight against mainstream society because "in their minds it undermines their values, the teachings of scripture as they interpret them, and the strength of the family" (175). Similarly, conservative Catholics use the issue of homosexuality to distinguish themselves from liberal Catholics, who have become more individualistic in their faith and less likely to uphold the moral authority of the church when it comes to making decisions about gender and sexuality (Konieczny 2013). Therefore, as mainline Protestants, liberal Catholics, and Americans in general become more accepting of gay and lesbian people and rights, conservative Christians maintain their embattled status by opposing civil rights for this population.

2

For the Bible
(or My Pastor/Priest) Tells Me So

The Bible and Homosexuality

I don't know if [scripture] means [gay and lesbian people] will
be separated from [God] forever or until they make a choice
in the very end, when all the dead in Christ rise ... to step away
from [homosexuality]. ... But I know that you can't live life as
a Christian and be a homosexual. It just doesn't work.
—Darlene, a twenty-six-year-old white evangelical
Protestant in central Mississippi

A Story from the Road

I was wide awake when my alarm went off at 6:30 a.m.; it was my
first full day of interviews. When I arrived at the church, I backed
my car in—a failed attempt to hide my feminist, gay and lesbian
rights, and Democratic bumper stickers. This was something I had
thought about the night before, but backing in was the best I could
do, as I had to park so that the interviewees could see where I was
located. My first interview of the morning went smoothly. Then
Candace and David arrived. Candace and David were a married
couple who attended Gulf Coast Nondenominational Church.
Both appeared to be white and in their early sixties. Candace was

very soft-spoken, yet her answers clearly showed the unwavering conservatism of her religious beliefs. David, on the other hand, was intense; throughout the entire interview, he stared at me intently and spoke aggressively, as if to indicate to me that I was his subordinate. He took a very patronizing tone during the interview.

As I asked David the last question of the interview, Candace walked into the doorway and waited. When the interview was over, she said she had thought of something else she would like to add to the last question of her interview. In reference to the question "Do programs created to change people's sexual orientation cause psychological distress?" Candace said she would like to add that even if such programs do cause psychological distress, it is not a bad thing. She explained, using verses from the Bible, that if people are sinning, then maybe psychological distress is necessary because it helps people see the error of their ways.

When their interviews were complete, David and Candace used the time to question me about my own beliefs. David asked, "Are you a Christian?" While I knew I would hear many conservative religious opinions (many of which I would not agree with) during my interviews, I was not prepared for the evangelism that was about to take place. I was not prepared for a direct attack on my personal beliefs and personhood.

There is debate over what is ethical and unethical behavior for qualitative researchers. Is it ethical to lie about my own beliefs, or should a researcher always tell the truth? How will my response influence my research? (Luckily, both of their interviews were already complete, but should I have needed to follow up with either of these respondents, I am sure my beliefs would have biased their responses.) I had considered these ethical dilemmas before embarking on the interview process, but these academic musings take on a new meaning when two people who have just condemned you to hell (along with all other gay and lesbian people) are confronting you. I decided I had to tell them the truth: "I do not identify as a Christian."

David and Candace continued to stare at me as if I were a specimen under a microscope. Then Candace pulled up a chair; I was practically trapped in the room and locked in their horrified yet sympathetic gazes. As I attempted to clarify my beliefs, they explained to me that Jesus is the only way to salvation. This was a segue into a conversation about the Trinity (a Christian doctrine that holds that God presents in three persons: Father, Son, and Holy Ghost). Subsequently, the mansplaining began. David, talking to me as if I were a two-year-old child, said, "Think of it like a malt chocolate milkshake. It's still three things—malt, chocolate, and ice cream—but they come together to make a whole." Candace chimed in, "It's like marriage. David and I are two separate people, but in marriage we came together as one to make a whole."

With heightened concern, they continued, "What about the Bible? It tells us that Jesus is God and that all of this is true. Do you not believe the Bible?" I explained, "I believe the Bible is an important book for Christians that provides moral guidance and is historically accurate in some parts but should not be taken literally." My skepticism led to a number of stories to prove the historical accuracy of the Bible. David told me about the "real" Mount Sinai (where Moses received the Ten Commandments, not the place the world knows as Mount Sinai) in the format of an adventure story that ended with Moses's friends finding the real Mount Sinai. Both David and Candace continued to stare at me fixedly as tears welled up in David's eyes.

Realizing his story had not converted me to his version of Christianity, David proceeded with the next archeological adventure through the Middle East. This one was a combination of the Exodus and the parting of the Red Sea. He told me how God parted the Red Sea and how "scientists" found the remnants of the Egyptians' chariots at the bottom of the Red Sea. He told me I could take a submarine ride down there to see for myself, but "of course all of the wood is gone so it's just old wheels." The final story, sure to convince me of the historical accuracy of the Bible, was about dinosaurs and humans inhabiting the earth simultaneously: "Scientists found a large rock underwater with a dinosaur track on it, and in the middle was a human footprint." In David's view, this clearly proved that evolution is a lie and creationism is the true story. These stories continued for over forty-five minutes.

I politely thanked them again for their time and stood to indicate this interview was over. Candace made a final attempt to save my soul by suggesting I read a book she had recommended to her son when he was also "questioning God." They both assured me there was a God and that Jesus was the only way to salvation in order to avoid an eternity in hell. I began to walk toward the door; I had just experienced the most intense attempt at evangelism in my life, and I was exhausted. They left, seemingly disappointed but optimistic that their attempt to save me would be fruitful in the long run.

I relay this story because I believe it clearly shows the importance of religion to many conservative Christians and their genuine belief that there is truly only one path to salvation. This story may be extreme, but it is not unique. Many conservative Christians, especially evangelicals, feel it is their duty to help others find the "Truth," their absolute truth. It is this strong conviction in a singular "Truth" that leads many people to view conservative Christians as close minded. Many conservative Christians refuse to accept any truth that does not fit into their religious worldview; for them, these contradictory truths must be rejected and eliminated. Candace and David ostensibly had my best interest at heart when they were trying to convince me to see the world through their particular lens. Especially for conservative Christians, the Bible (or at least what they believe the Bible says based on their pastor's, priest's, or denomination's interpretation) shapes the lens through which they view the entire world.

It is also important to note that most respondents did not realize they were devaluing me personally. The majority of respondents assumed I was heterosexual and Protestant. Many respondents spoke in terms of "us" (me and the respondent) versus "them" (gay and lesbian people). They assumed I held the same or similar religious beliefs as they did. For example, one Catholic respondent explained, "I'm not Protestant, so I'm not a memorize-the-Bible kind of person like *you guys* do. *You guys* are so good at that" (emphasis added). Respondents made these assumptions despite the fact that I did not reveal anything about myself to them before they completed their interviews.

Mississippi Christians' Interpretations and Beliefs about the Bible

How Christians interpret the Bible plays a significant role in their understanding of social issues, specifically gay and lesbian rights. Using the same primary text, Christians across denominations and wider religious categories (e.g., evangelical versus mainline) have arrived at extremely different understandings of what it means to be a Christian. For most Christians, the Bible is a framework and guidebook for living a moral life. Across religious categories and denominations, the Bible is considered by most adherents to be a significant guide to life as a Christian. The majority of respondents agreed that being a true Christian meant that one must believe the Bible is infallible. But Christians often diverge on how the Bible should be read and interpreted. The study of interpretation, hermeneutics, attempts to make sense of how individuals reading the same text can arrive at such divergent meanings.

According to hermeneutic theory, "it's expected that different readers will arrive at discrepant interpretations of a given text, and that purveyors of competing interpretations may attempt to marshal various forms of evidence (e.g., scientific, experiential, ethical) to lend legitimacy to their particular reading of the text in question" (Bartkowski 1996, 262). These discrepant interpretations primarily arise from two of the diverse characteristics that readers bring to the text: (1) readers' "biases or 'prejudices' which are often conditioned by their social, historical, and cultural location . . . [and] the reader's taken-for-granted assumptions often are revealed in the act of reading"; and (2) readers' attempts to "employ a circular interpretive strategy—the 'hermeneutic circle'—to ascribe coherent meaning to the text and its constitute parts" (Bartkowski 1996, 262). Overall, Christians bring their assumptions about human nature and the Bible with them to their interpretation of the text itself. By trying to reconcile the text with their previous assumptions and make contradictory stories and passages fit together, interpretations of the Bible vary based on the reader. Clearly, these assumptions about human nature and the Bible are also largely influenced by the pastor or priest who is responsible for being the expert on the core text of Christianity.

There are at least two ways to think about biblical interpretation. The first and most often used strategy of understanding different biblical interpretations regards how the text is viewed. Does the reader view the text as infallible, inspired, inerrant, literal, and so on? Second, using a hermeneutic lens, biblical interpretation is based on the reader's biases and their belief about the overall message of the Bible.

The evangelical Protestants in this study argued that the Bible should be interpreted literally. This belief in biblical literalism is based on the premise that God does not make mistakes; therefore, the Bible is without error. Many evangelical Protestants, and some conservative Catholics, felt that there was only one true meaning of scripture that should be apparent from reading the text literally. In contrast, more liberal Christians in this study usually viewed the Bible as a set of guidelines for living but did not suggest it was without error or must be taken literally.

The most frequent terminology interviewees used to discuss the Bible included "the inspired word of God," "infallible," "inerrant," and "literal within context." While the words *infallible* and *inerrant* seem to hold similar meanings, these nuanced terms can be used to imply very different understandings of the Bible. *Infallible* is used to mean that the Bible is incapable of mistake. Respondents who use this term are not necessarily arguing that there are no errors in the Bible; rather, the term indicates that the overall message of the Bible is not mistaken. Hence even if historical, logical, or typographical errors are present in the Bible, the message is clear. *Inerrancy*, meanwhile, argues there are no errors or contradictions in the writing or facts of the Bible. Consequently, it is possible to believe the Bible is infallible without believing it is inerrant. However, the belief that the Bible is inerrant implies infallibility.

Despite differences in terminology, many Christians use the terms *inerrancy* and *infallibility* interchangeably. Another closely related phrase is *biblical literalism*, which is used to mean that biblical passages should be interpreted at face value. While most conservative Christians believe all three—that the Bible is infallible, inerrant, and meant to be interpreted literally—more moderate and liberal Christians usually move away from biblical literalism and inerrancy. Many Christians in this study believed that the Bible, or at least the message of the Bible, is infallible or incapable of mistake, but it was only the more conservative Christians who believed the actual text is without error or contradiction and only the *most* conservative Christians who believed all passages in the Bible should be taken literally.

Some respondents in this study also used the phrase *literal within context*. Literal within context may sound like an oxymoron, but to the interviewees in this study, it made perfect sense. When using this phrase, the interviewees were attempting to explain that the Bible should be read at face value but that the reading must nevertheless be understood within the historical context in which the Bible was written. Interpretation of the text is not necessary, but interpretation of the context in which that text was written is needed to truly understand a passage.

No matter how respondents interpreted the Bible, they felt their interpretations were consistent and without bias or prejudice, but as hermeneutic theory makes clear, interpreting anything without bias is difficult if not impossible. While most Christians, and especially Protestants, did suggest their interpretation is based on how they read the Bible, the respondents' answers in this study show that the importance of bias and the perceived overall message of the Bible play much greater roles in interpretation than literalism or inerrancy alone. For example, Bartkowski (1996) found that even among conservative Christians who subscribe to a literal interpretation of the Bible, it is possible to arrive at very different conclusions. This is why Bartkowski (1996) argues that there are "problems associated with describing conservative Protestant biblical interpretations merely in terms of 'inerrancy' or 'literalism'" (269).

Additionally, as respondents began to explain their biblical beliefs about homosexuality, it became obvious that the common texts thought to comment on the topic of homosexuality were interpreted to align with respondents' overall beliefs about the meaning of the Bible—an example of the hermeneutic circle. For example, if the respondent believed the overall message of the Bible is to love one another and not pass judgment, then they interpreted certain Bible verses used by others to condemn homosexuality as not regarding (or at least not condemning) a loving and monogamous same-sex relationship. If, however, the respondent felt that the overall purpose of the Bible is to explain to Christians how to live a life without sinning and that sin leads to destruction, then they interpreted the same Bible verses to be a condemnation of homosexuality. Whether Christians believe their interpretation of the Bible is infallible, inerrant, or literal does not matter as much as their beliefs about human nature and the purpose of the Bible.

In order to demonstrate these various ways of thinking about interpretation, I examine how respondents talked about interpreting the Bible and provide an overview of the six key passages many Christians use to discuss homosexuality. After discussing the six key passages, I explore how respondents in this study used the Bible to justify their beliefs about homosexuality. There are apparent discrepancies between respondents' explanations of how they interpreted the Bible and their actual interpretations of what the Bible says about homosexuality. Respondents' values, biases, and prejudices concerning the overall message of the Bible became extremely clear when they discussed the issue of homosexuality and the Bible.

WHAT ARE YOUR BELIEFS ABOUT THE BIBLE?

Kelsey, a thirty-two-year-old white mainline Protestant pastor in south-central Mississippi, explained, "I think [the Bible] should be taken literally, but I think that you have to . . . take into account their intentions and what it was about when it was written and the genre." Multiple interviewees mentioned the importance of genre or writing style. By this they were suggesting that if the story were written to be an allegory or fable, to take it as fact would not be correct. According to them, inconsistencies or unbelievable stories in the Bible do not mean the Bible is not meant to be taken literally; rather, it suggests that these stories were written in a different format for a different purpose. Kelsey went on to say that she thinks the Bible is inerrant and then clarified her definition of inerrant: "To me it means that it's God's word, and God doesn't mess up on that. Are there editing mistakes? Yes. Are their contradictions? Yes." Like Kelsey, many respondents felt that understanding and interpreting the Bible is not a straightforward process. Although Kelsey believed God's message is inerrant, this did not mean the Bible itself is without mistakes.

Most respondents interviewed held complex views about biblical interpretation that fell somewhere between the two extremes of completely inerrant and literal interpretation versus interpretation as a book of stories. The bulk of interviewees agreed with Victor, a forty-three-year-old white mainline Protestant in northeast Mississippi, who thought the Bible is "basically a written record of God's account of how we are to live our lives." The terminology used and the beliefs about biblical inerrancy largely fell along the lines of religious identification. While all evangelical Protestants interviewed claimed that the Bible is the inerrant word of God, only four of the eleven Catholics and seven of the nineteen mainline Protestants used this terminology when asked to share their beliefs about the Bible.

Interview respondents' religious affiliations were even more influential when it came to the issue of biblical literalism. The majority of both mainline Protestants and Catholics interviewed agreed that the Bible should not be taken literally. Of the nineteen mainline Protestants, thirteen indicated the Bible should not be read literally. In fact, only one mainline Protestant suggested the Bible should *always* be taken literally. Nine of the eleven Catholics agreed the Bible should not be taken literally. On the opposite end of the spectrum, however, eight of the ten evangelical Protestants explained the Bible must be taken literally. As Regina, an evangelical Baptist, explained, the Bible is "totally truth."

Despite the nuances, mainline Protestants and Catholics agreed more closely on how the Bible should be understood and interpreted than did Catholics and evangelical Protestants. Where Catholics *did* diverge from mainline Protestants is that some Catholics felt that the Bible is not for laypeople to interpret at all. Manning (1999) explains that within the Catholic Church, conservatives and liberals are divided over where they locate moral authority. She describes a conservative Catholic as "one who accepts the authority of the magisterium [the authority of the pope and bishops within the Catholic Church to define the church's authentic teachings] and feels that a good Catholic should be obedient to all church teachings" (64–65). On the other hand, a liberal Catholic "questions the church, locates authority in herself [or himself], and only selectively adheres to church doctrine" (65). Based on this understanding, most Catholics in this study fall into the conservative category—that is, they felt it was the church, not individuals, who had the authority to interpret the Bible. This belief clearly differed from that of most Protestants, who contended that individual laypeople have the ability to interpret and understand the Bible. This difference also led to a different emphasis being placed on the Bible by Catholics and Protestants.

The belief that the Bible should not be interpreted by laypeople led many Catholics in this study to feel a lack of connection to the Bible. They expressed difficulty in understanding the Bible outside of the interpretation of the Catholic Church. For example, Hillary, a fifty-three-year-old white Catholic from northeast Mississippi, described, "There is really one interpretation of the Bible. . . . It's meant to be the truth. It's meant to be a certain thing, not for all to interpret it in the way it speaks to us. That's why I'm Catholic." Hillary was clear: the Bible is not meant to be taken literally in all places, and it is the authority of the Vatican to define the one true meaning of the Bible. (It is important to decipher between this one true interpretation she speaks of and evangelical

Protestants' belief in a literal interpretation of the Bible.) Along the same lines, Brenda, a forty-four-year-old white Catholic from the Gulf Coast, said, "This might be the Catholic [in me] . . . I just don't feel connected to the Bible." Likewise, when I asked Kristina, a thirty-six-year-old white Catholic from northeast Mississippi, what the Bible says about homosexuality, she indicated she did not know, then continued, "I'm resorting back to [the notion] that the Catholics don't know the Bible like they should [excuse]."

These findings are important because D'Antonio et al. (2013) showed most Catholics today do not feel the Catholic Church's authority is necessary. Therefore, the Mississippi Catholics interviewed in this study fall into the minority of Catholics across the United States, who continue to rely on the Vatican's teaching authority, and not their own authority, to interpret scripture and church doctrine. This does not mean the Mississippi Catholics in this study did not find the Bible important; rather, they relied on the authority of the Catholic Church to interpret the meaning for them. Even for those who "don't know the Bible like they should," the Bible was still an important guide for living. Whether the respondents in this study read the Bible directly or had it interpreted for them by their denomination, pastor, or priest, the Bible was at the core of their understanding of religion. With this understanding of respondents' beliefs about the Bible in mind, I now turn to an examination of what Mississippi Christians believe the Bible says about homosexuality.

THE BIBLE AND HOMOSEXUALITY

There are six primary biblical passages that have been used to condemn homosexuality within Christianity. Three of these passages are found in the Old Testament, and three are found in the New Testament. I use the King James Version (KJV) of these Bible passages because, as *Christianity Today* reports, according to data collected from the General Social Survey and the National Congregations Survey, the KJV is the most highly read Bible in the United States today (Zylstra 2014). Of Bible readers, 55 percent report using the KJV Bible, compared to the 19 percent who use the New International Version (NIV), the second-most popular translation of the Bible (Zylstra 2014). All other versions of the Bible have readership percentages in the single digits (Zylstra 2014). I footnote where there are major discrepancies in language between the KJV, the NIV, and the New American Bible (Revised Edition) (NABRE), because each translation is associated with different religious affiliations. The KJV has been predominantly associated with evangelical Protestant traditions, while the NIV, the NABRE (used in Catholic mass in the United States), and other translations are more widely used in mainline Protestant and Catholic traditions.

The most widely quoted biblical condemnation of homosexuality is the story of Sodom and Gomorrah, from Genesis 19:

> 1 And there came two angels to Sodom at evening; and Lot sat in the gate of Sodom: and Lot seeing them rose up to meet them; and he bowed himself with his face toward the ground; 2 And he said, behold now, my lords, turn in, I pray you, into your servant's house, and tarry all night, and wash your feet, and ye shall rise up early, and go on your ways. And they said, Nay; but we will abide in the street all night. 3 And he pressed upon them greatly; and they turned in unto him, and entered into his house; and he made them a feast, and did bake unleavened bread, and they did eat. 4 But before they lay down, the men of the city, even the men of Sodom, compassed the house round, both old and young, all the people from every quarter: 5 And they called unto Lot, and said unto him, Where are the men which came in to thee this night? Bring them out unto us, that we may know them.[1] 6 And Lot went out at the door unto them, and shut the door after him, 7 And said, I pray you, brethren, do not so wickedly. 8 Behold now, I have two daughters which have not known man; let me, I pray you, bring them out unto you, and do ye to them as is good in your eyes: only unto these men do nothing; for therefore came they under the shadow of my roof. 9 And they said, Stand back.

And they said again, This one fellow came in to sojourn, and he will needs be a judge: now will we deal worse with thee, than with them. And they pressed sore upon the man, even Lot, and came near to break the door. 10 But the men put forth their hand, and pulled Lot into the house to them, and shut to the door. 11 And they smote the men that were at the door of the house with blindness, both small and great: so that they wearied themselves to find the door. 12 And the men said unto Lot, Hast thou here any besides? Son in law, and thy sons, and thy daughters, and whatsoever thou hast in the city, bring them out of this place: 13 For we will destroy this place, because the cry of them is waxen great before the face of the Lord; and the Lord hath sent us to destroy it.

Many evangelical Protestants argue that a literal interpretation of this passage makes it clear that God destroyed the city of Sodom because the men had sex with other men. The men refused to have sex with Lot's daughters and instead attempted to force themselves upon Lot's male guests. Upon reading these passages, many evangelical Protestants surmise that the homosexual acts that occurred led to the destruction of the city. While other interpretations of this passage suggest it could have been the lack of hospitality or other sins that led to the destruction of Sodom,[2] evangelical Protestants are generally adamant that men having sex with other men is the main sin that occurred in the story of Sodom and Gomorrah.[3]

In addition to this passage, Leviticus 18:22 and 20:13 are used as justification for condemning same-sex sexuality. Leviticus is one of two books of law in the Old Testament; it provides regulations and laws for Jews and explains the rituals and practices necessary to live a moral life. Leviticus 18:22 reads, "Thou shalt not lie with mankind, as with womankind: it is abomination." Leviticus 20:13 states, "If a man also lie with mankind, as he lieth with a woman, both of them have committed an abomination: they shall surely be put to death; their blood shall be upon them."[4] Some interpret these scriptures to mean that if a man has any type of sexual relationship with another man instead of with a woman, both men are sinning against God and will suffer the consequences of these sins—death.

While these passages from Leviticus seem more straightforward than the story of Sodom and Gomorrah, many Christians question their meaning and how they should be understood in a modern context. The differing interpretations of these particular passages from Leviticus arise for various reasons. One reason is that different translations use distinctive language. For instance, the NIV translation's use of "detestable," rather than "abomination," changes the meaning of the passage. The word *detestable* clearly has different connotations than the word *abomination*, although it is also unclear how *abomination* should be interpreted. While some Christians suggest it is synonymous with "sin," others argue that it means separation from God rather than the breaking of the law of God.

Another reason some Christians question the validity of these verses to condemn homosexuality is the belief that Jesus's laws in the New Testament replace those in the Old Testament. Christians today do not follow many of the laws in Leviticus or Deuteronomy, such as the laws that prohibit eating shellfish or wearing clothing made of two different materials. Consequently, some Christians argue that picking and choosing which laws to follow from the Old Testament does not make sense and that Christians today must look to the New Testament for guidance.

In the New Testament, three passages are typically interpreted to justify condemnation of homosexuality: Romans 1:26, 1 Corinthians 6:9, and 1 Timothy 1:10. All three of these books are attributed to the apostle Paul. In Romans, Paul explains to Rome his theological beliefs and how to live life as a Christian. First Corinthians is a letter to a church Paul founded in Corinth explaining the time has come for the church members to turn away from their sins. First Timothy is the first of two letters from Paul to one of his delegates in Ephesus, Timothy, and provides instructions for leading his church.

Romans 1:26 states, "For this cause God gave them up unto vile affections: for even their women did change the natural use into that which is against nature."[5] While this passage does not directly mention homosexuality, many evangelical Christians interpret it to mean that both men and women gave into their sexual desires for the same sex and these desires were against nature, and therefore against God.

First Corinthians 6:9 reads, "Know ye not that the unrighteous shall not inherit the kingdom of God? Be not deceived: neither fornicators, nor idolaters, nor adulterers, nor effeminate, nor abusers of themselves with mankind."[6] The NIV version of the text specifically mentions men who have sex with other men, while the NABRE translation uses the phrase "boy prostitutes." In this passage, Paul is warning his church that sex outside of heterosexual, monogamous marriages is prohibited and will result in the punishment of not inheriting God's kingdom. While this is a clear prohibition of homosexuality to conservative Christians, it has also been suggested that this passage is actually condemning sex between adult men and boys. At that time in history, it was not uncommon for adult men to have sex with young boys. Hence many suggest that this passage is not a blanket condemnation of homosexuality but rather only a condemnation of the rape of young boys. Some Christians suggest that no passages in the New Testament condemn consensual same-sex relationships between adults.

The final verse used to condemn homosexuality in the New Testament is 1 Timothy 1:10. This verse explains that laws are made not for innocent people but rather "for whoremongers, for them that defile themselves with mankind, for menstealers,[7] for liars, for perjured persons, and if there be any other thing that is contrary to sound doctrine." The NIV translation of the Bible uses the word *homosexuality* in this verse, but the term was not actually used in discourse until around the year 1850. Based on this, some Christians suggest that to translate the text this way is a clear error, since today's idea of homosexuality is fairly new. Of course, men had sex with other men at this time, but the way we think about homosexuality (or sexuality more generally) today would not have been understood. This is another reason that some Christians discredit the interpretation of these texts as prohibiting same-sex relationships.

Overall, in these New Testament passages, Paul condemns those who trade "natural" sexual relations with women for those with men. Many Christians believe that these three verses are a clear warning to Paul's churches that those who do not follow God's intentions for sex—a man and a woman having sex for the purpose of procreation—will not go to heaven. On the other hand, many mainline Protestants and liberal Catholics disagree with these interpretations and feel that consensual relationships between two people of the same sex are not specifically prohibited in the Bible.

WHAT THE BIBLE MEANS ABOUT HOMOSEXUALITY

The interpretations of these stories and passages are important for understanding Christians' views about homosexuality. Many respondents believed that Christians must take both the Old and New Testament passages literally, which suggested to them that same-sex relations are always sinful and against the will of God. All the evangelical Christians interviewed argued that homosexuality is always sinful according to the Bible. Most (eight of ten) relied on both Old and New Testament scriptures to support this argument. Two evangelical interviewees explained that Jesus had already fulfilledthe Old Testament (Jesus's return having brought about a new law), and therefore they based their beliefs about homosexuality being sinful on Paul's letters in the New Testament. In addition to the evangelical Protestants interviewed, almost half (five of eleven) of Catholics also agreed that the Bible says homosexuality is always sinful. In comparison, only two mainline Protestants felt that homosexuality was always sinful.

The respondents who felt that the Old Testament passages were no longer relevant to modern-day Christianity believed that Jesus had already fulfilled the scriptures and made the old laws obsolete. This interpretation is largely derived from Hebrews 8:13 and Romans 10:4. For instance, Brad, a fifty-six-year-old white mainline Protestant from the Gulf Coast of Mississippi, explained that Christians today are "more New Testament people." Based on the same belief, four Catholic and four mainline Protestant interviewees argued that the Bible says little or nothing about homosexuality as we know it today. They reasoned that the passages used to justify opposition to homosexuality were not meant to condemn loving same-sex relationships. These interviewees explained that the Bible was written in a specific historical context, and therefore must be interpreted accordingly. For example, Barbara, a fifty-five-year-old white mainline Protestant from northeast Mississippi, explained:

> Overall, I think a lot of the guidelines from the Old Testament, such as not sleeping with the same sex, are put there for health reasons . . . and for the continuance of the population and procreation. I believe also that God is against promiscuity, whether you're straight or homosexual, and I think God wants us to be in monogamous relationships. . . . I just don't think it's biblically correct either to select a certain segment of society and be so rejectful of them in general. . . . To me, [the Bible] has scriptures against [homosexuality], but I don't think it has any more consequence than the scriptures against having meat products with milk products because you could end up with a disease. I just think it was for practical purposes.

While Barbara conceded that the Bible has passages that could be interpreted to condemn homosexuality, she argued these passages were written at a specific time in history and are no longer relevant to our modern-day lives. She believed that the Bible prohibits same-sex relationships for health reasons only; therefore, if same-sex couples are having safe (and for her, monogamous) sex, then the Bible says nothing about this being sinful.

On the other hand, Ervin, a fifty-five-year-old black mainline Protestant from central Mississippi, felt that Jesus fulfilled some of the laws of the Old Testament, such as the obligation to sacrifice animals or to be circumcised, but that the laws about homosexuality remain unchanged. Ervin explained:

> I think the Bible is pretty clear on homosexuality. . . . Leviticus talks specifically about homosexuality being an abomination. . . . When [God] gets to homosexuality, or what we call homosexuality, he specifically says that a man should not lie with a male as with a woman. . . . So, to me that's very clear, I don't see any other way of interpreting that other than the Bible saying, or specifically [God's] saying, don't do these things. . . . God is sending people and having his prophets and messengers and angels and different people to say "don't do these things," and so from that standpoint, I don't think that I'm misinterpreting that at all in saying essentially, "No homosexuality."

Andrew, an evangelical Protestant, seemed to agree. He told me the "ceremonial laws are fulfilled in Christ," but he still used the Old Testament as evidence that homosexuality is sinful.

Some of the respondents in this study argued that Jesus's commandments to love and not judge one another outweighed the few verses of scripture that speak about homosexuality. These respondents clearly demonstrated the importance of the hermeneutic circle in biblical interpretation. They used their overall belief in love to interpret the meaning of specific passages that could be used to condemn homosexuality. Approximately half (nine of nineteen) of mainline Protestants and some Catholic respondents explained the overarching theme of the Bible is to love one another and leave judgment to God. Casey, a mainline Protestant, described her feelings about the issue when she said, "I feel like you have to look at the Bible and its message as a whole, and Jesus's life and what he left us and apply those. So, what do I feel like the Bible says about homosexuality? I feel like the Bible tells us that every person is a child of God and every person should be loved equally." Similarly, Isabelle, a seventy-five-year-old black mainline Protestant in central Mississippi, explained, "God has to be the judge . . . and any of us sitting in the church wanting to deny someone because they're homeless, homosexual, or black, or white, then we shouldn't be there either." Rick, a Catholic, agreed with Isabelle. He stated, "I'm very hesitant [to state an opinion] because I'm not God, and I have absolutely no intention to judge whether someone else is in a state of sin or not because I don't know that person's conscience." The interviewees who felt that the overarching message of love was more important than individual Bible verses did not confirm or deny the validity of the six biblical passages used to condemn homosexuality. To them this was a moot point. These mainline Protestants felt that pulling six Bible verses out of the entire Bible and allowing them to override love and nonjudgment defeated the goal and purpose of Christianity.

This is not to say evangelical Protestants who believe homosexuality is a sin or those who believe homosexuality is sinful more broadly are ignoring biblical passages about love and nonjudgment. In reality, both groups indicated that it was love that led them to hold their position so strongly. Those who argued that homosexuality is sinful suggested it was from a position of compassion that they preached the "Truth" and that it was because of this compassion that they felt it was important to help those "struggling" with homosexuality. More conservative Christians' hermeneutic circle (based on sin and punishment) led them to believe the only way to interpret the scriptures and to "save" gay and lesbian people was to help them realize their sin and overcome it. For example, Candace, the evangelical Protestant introduced at the beginning of this chapter, argued, "I think it's so important for Christians to be able to reach out in love to anybody who is walking in sin, because if you see someone who is caught in a trap and you don't make an effort to help them get out, then what kind of love is that?" Erica, an evangelical Protestant, agreed; she explained that her church's position on homosexuality is "the same as the Bible's position. Love people, but tell them the truth. Tell them the truth and love."

The role of love is an extremely important caveat because evangelical Protestants are often painted as approaching the issue of homosexuality out of irrational hate or fear. Evangelical Protestants interviewed for this study often displayed an intense fear surrounding the issue of homosexuality, but most answers did not seem to come from a place of hatred or a desire to punish gay and lesbian people. Rather, many evangelical Protestants, who wholly opposed homosexuality, felt that it was truly in the best interests of gay and lesbian people to tell them they were sinning and to help them overcome this sin. When the topic of homosexuality is viewed through an evangelical Protestant lens, their stance seems more consistent and internally rational. Since evangelical Protestants believe that someone who does not turn away from sin (in this case, homosexuality) will suffer the consequences—that is, hell—it would indeed be in the best interests of gay and lesbian people that Christians attempt to discourage homosexuality and "save" gay and lesbian people from damnation. Seeing the world through this lens suggests that opposition to homosexuality can come from concern for the well-being of others.

In most matters in this study, Catholics' responses were in between those of evangelical Protestants and mainline Protestants. However, the interpretation of what the Bible says about homosexuality was one of the few cases where many Catholics more closely aligned with evangelical Protestants. As stated, over half the Catholics interviewed indicated that homosexuality is always sinful. Yet Catholics' views shifted back toward those of mainline Protestants when it came to how Christians should deal with the issue of gay and lesbian rights. Before turning to how Christians thought their churches should deal with gay and lesbian people, it will be helpful to examine which Bible verses the respondents in this study referenced when making the argument that homosexuality is a sin.

BY THE VERSE: MISSISSIPPI CHRISTIANS' USE OF THE BIBLE TO CONDEMN HOMOSEXUALITY

The majority of arguments against homosexuality in the United States today ultimately revolve around religion. Even in politics, where there is ostensibly a separation from religion, the major argument against gay and lesbian rights remains religious in nature.

Therefore, it is important to understand where Christians find justification for opposition to homosexuality and gay and lesbian rights.

Although many interview respondents indicated homosexuality is sinful and "against the will of God," most were unsure exactly what the Bible says about homosexuality. Over a quarter of interview respondents (eleven of forty) admitted that they did not know what the Bible actually says about homosexuality. Some respondents vaguely discussed Old Testament passages about homosexuality, while others indicated they believed Paul discussed the issue in the New Testament. Still, most admitted they could not point to a specific verse in scripture that discusses the topic. While the idea that homosexuality is sinful was prevalent among respondents, they struggled to explain why they held this belief. "For the Bible tells me so" may be a common refrain for Christians, but what the Bible actually says appears to be less clear. Many interviewees held that same-sex relations were not natural or what God intended, but the specifics of why were often lost in translation.

Many respondents in this study agreed that a prohibition of homosexuality could be found in the Old Testament. Twenty-three of the forty interviewees mentioned the Old Testament when discussing what the Bible says about homosexuality, though most did not know where in the Old Testament the verse(s) are found. Seven respondents indicated they believed there is some prohibition against homosexuality in either Deuteronomy or Leviticus, the books of law. Some mainline Protestants quoted or paraphrased Leviticus 18:22, yet they did not know the chapter or verse where the quote is located. Two evangelical Protestants mentioned the story of Adam and Eve to show homosexuality is not natural. For example, Angela, an evangelical Protestant, argued the prohibition of homosexuality began with Adam and Eve (Genesis 1; the first book and chapter of the Bible). She said, "The Lord tells us that he made Adam, and Eve for Adam, and he said that a man should not lust after another man nor a woman lust after another woman. And that's just going against what God has said in the Bible." All in all, respondents were sure the Old Testament says homosexuality is a sin, but where it says that was less clear.

Evangelical Protestants were the only respondents to mention books in the New Testament as prohibiting homosexuality. The books they indicated were Romans, 1 and 2 Corinthians, and 1 Timothy. One evangelical respondent, Darlene, paraphrased 1 Corinthians 6:9, which she interpreted to mean that gay and lesbian people will not inherit the kingdom of God. She explained, "It's in a number of places . . . it says in one part that those who practice homosexuality cannot inherit the kingdom of God . . . it says that you can't be a believer and follow that because . . . being a Christian you inherit the kingdom of God. How can you inherit [the kingdom of God] if you're doing exactly what it says you cannot? . . . [Also,] Paul talks a lot about it, I think it's in Corinthians . . . it's in a couple of the letters." A few other respondents indicated they believed Paul mentions homosexuality in a letter but were not sure where it is in the Bible.

Some mainline Protestants and Catholics indicated they did not know of any place in the Bible that speaks directly to the issue of what we call homosexuality today. Five mainline Protestants and three Catholics explained that the Bible does not directly address the issue of homosexuality; no evangelical Protestants agreed with this position. Kelsey, a mainline Protestant, told me that the Old Testament speaks about homosexuality but that "Jesus didn't even mention homosexuality. I think it was more of a nonissue. . . . Everybody is created in the image of God, and also it doesn't really give us a clear answer on why are people homosexual, or are they really." Phillip, a seventy-one-year-old white Catholic from northeast Mississippi, also felt that the Bible does not have a lot to say about homosexuality. He believed that the Old Testament mentions it, but he largely agreed with Kelsey that it was a "nonissue." Phillip explained, "There's a lot of one-liners in the Old Testament about sexuality that have to be taken pretty much in context, but overall I'm not all that aware of many things in scripture that address homosexuality blatantly unless you go into the Old Testament and find some things during the time of the ancient Hebrew life that have some words about it." Along the same lines, Rick, a forty-three-year-old white Catholic interviewee from northeast Mississippi, said he did not think the Bible has anything to say about homosexuality; rather, he believed "what the Bible does is it gives us a framework within which our own sexuality can be rightly expressed and that framework would be within marriage, but does it say anything about homosexual persons per say or homosexuality? No."

In contrast to most of the mainline Protestants and Catholics I interviewed, one Catholic respondent, Hillary, had taken time to examine what the Bible specifically says about homosexuality. She told me she did not have the verses memorized but had a list of all the verses she could read to me. She explained, "I'm not Protestant, so I'm not a memorize-the-Bible kind of person. . . . But I've got like a kind of listing here, I've got a little cheat sheet here." Hillary went on to list Leviticus 18:22, Leviticus 20:13, Deuteronomy 22:5 ("Do not wear opposite sex clothing"), Jude 1:7 (which discusses Sodom and Gomorrah, citing "how they gave themselves up to several immoralities, how they gave themselves up to sexual immoralities and perversion"), and Romans 1:24–27 ("Men committed indecent acts with other men and received in themselves the due penalty for their perversion").

Whereas most respondents were unsure of any Bible verses prohibiting homosexuality, others cited more than the typical verses listed above. Similar to Hillary, however, these few individuals usually conflated gender and sexuality. For instance, the passage pointed out above, Deuteronomy 22:5, is about wearing the "opposite sex's clothing." Obviously, this respondent believed dressing in opposite-sex clothing means a person is gay or lesbian. To the contrary, research shows that most cross-dressers identify as heterosexual (Docter and Prince 1997). Also, one evangelical Protestant explained that many verses speak of "the feminine." She implied that men acting feminine equated to homosexuality in the Bible. This makes sense when considering the strong relationship between conservative Christians' gender ideology and their condemnation of homosexuality (Gallagher 2004; Konieczny 2013).

Overall, this lack of specificity regarding what the Bible actually says about homosexuality may not be as surprising for mainline Protestants and Catholics. Generally, these two groups either do not find the Bible as essential to their beliefs or feel that it is not within their authority to interpret. Conversely, the fact that many evangelical Protestants were unsure what the Bible says about homosexuality seems more unexpected, at least at first glance. Evangelical Protestants' belief that everyone can and should both read and understand the Bible, combined with their staunch opposition to homosexuality, would suggest that they would be more aware of certain biblical passages than the data in this study indicate. Despite evangelical Protestants' ideological positions on the Bible, this study supports previous research showing that evangelical Protestants may be much more like mainline Protestants and Catholics when it comes to interpreting the Bible than is often assumed. In fact, it appears that, like mainline Protestants and Catholics, many evangelical Protestants rely on their pastor for understanding the Bible rather than their own individual readings of the Bible (Bartkowski 1996). Overall, I found that most respondents' beliefs relied more heavily on the teachings and authority of their denomination or pastor/priest than directly on the Bible itself.

I GET IT FROM MY . . . PASTOR

Respondents largely appeared to trust their denomination's stance or their pastor/priest's interpretation of the Bible on the issues of homosexuality and gay and lesbian rights. As previously mentioned, conservative Catholics often base their opposition to same-sex marriage on the Catholic Church's stance on gender and sexuality, which indicates that sexual intimacy is only for the purpose of reproduction within marriage (Konieczny 2013). Additionally, research has shown that Protestants also place a lot of faith in their pastors' or churches' stance on the Bible. For instance, Bartkowski (1996) explains that "viable conservative Protestant scriptural readings are not generated through individual study of the Bible, but via the *interpretive community* in which the individual evangelical is situated. From this perspective, the interpretive community—under the leadership of its interpretive authorities such as pastors and theologians—determines the 'ground rules' for scriptural interpretation" (270; emphasis in original). Based on this research, it makes sense that most respondents do not know exactly what the Bible says about homosexuality, because they have learned these messages through their interpretive community, not through individual study of the Bible itself. Some respondents clearly admitted that they allowed their pastor or priest to interpret the Bible for them.

Tim, a forty-year-old white Catholic from northeast Mississippi, said, "I haven't actually read [what the Bible says], but I mean I've always been taught that [homosexuality] is wrong." Similarly, Whitney, a fifty-two-year-old white Catholic woman living in northeast Mississippi, told me she believes being homosexual is not sinful, but acting on same-sex desires is a sin. When I asked her where in scripture it says homosexual acts are sinful, she responded, "I know there are scripture passages . . . [but] I'm not a real big quote-scripture-remember-scripture-verbatim girl." Again, it was not just Catholics who took this approach. Regina, an evangelical Protestant, told me homosexuality is "not the norm" and that she believes it is a sin. Yet when I asked Regina to provide a biblical justification for this belief, she said, "I don't concentrate on that. All I do is the love of God."

In fact, only a handful of respondents indicated that they held beliefs that were *not* directly in line with their church's position on the issues of homosexuality and gay and lesbian rights. One such respondent was Leo, a sixty-year-old white mainline Protestant in northeast Mississippi, who stated that his church is "evolving." He continued, "The church, I believe, wants to find ways to grow and it wants to find a way of doing what we've always said we do, which is that we accept all persons and all persons are children of Jesus Christ, regardless of their backgrounds." Even though his church is changing, Leo believed his views about homosexuality were more progressive than his church's current position. Likewise, Marie, a sixty-nine-year-old white mainline Protestant in northeast Mississippi, explained that even though she would like to think her church feels the same way she does about homosexuality, one situation made her think she may have a different opinion about the topic than her church. She described the situation this way: "A gay man that I know wanted to go into the priesthood and our bishop advised him not to. . . . I think they should have accepted him and encouraged him to join the priesthood." These responses were the exceptions to the rule; most interviewees said they thought or hoped their views were the same as their church's position on the issue of homosexuality. Despite the fact that most respondents felt they agreed with their churches' respective positions, it is clear from the interviews that this may not always have been the reality, since even when respondents held an opposing view to another member of their congregation, they continued to believe theirs was the view of their pastor/priest and their church at large.

Obviously, homosexuality is a contentious issue in Christian churches, especially in Mississippi. Even within the same congregation, the members surveyed held conflicting views and beliefs about the topic. When we look across religious ideologies and affiliations, these divides become even greater.

Despite where beliefs about homosexuality originate, these beliefs still raise an interesting dilemma and position today's Christians in two opposing factions. On one side are those who condemn homosexuality and believe it is Christians' duty to teach others about the sinfulness of homosexuality; on the other, those who believe Christians must accept gay and lesbian people with open arms. So what does this mean for Christian churches, and how does this division influence Christians' beliefs about one another?

HOW SHOULD CHURCHES HANDLE THE ISSUE OF HOMOSEXUALITY?

When discussing how Christians should handle the issue of homosexuality, many respondents seemed uncertain. Most agreed that gay and lesbian people should be welcomed into their respective churches, but the degree of acceptance and the reasons for such a welcome varied. For evangelical Protestant interviewees, welcoming gay and lesbian people into Christian churches was a way to reach them and attempt to change their behaviors. Eight of the ten evangelical Protestants interviewed said they would welcome gay and lesbian people to attend their church in order to help them understand that their behavior is sinful and repent of this sin. Angela explained it like this: "I guess we should welcome them with loving arms . . . therefore they . . . grow closer to the Lord. Then they would hopefully learn more about God's word and that this [homosexual] lifestyle is a sin. Then they would hopefully turn from that [sin] and want to please the Lord and not do that anymore." Clearly, this welcome is conditional and with an agenda; Angela wants to welcome gay and lesbian people in order to save them from their sinful "lifestyle." Another evangelical Protestant, Andrew, believed anyone should be welcomed at his church, "but in terms of to be considered a member, I think there needs to be an acknowledgment of biblical standards of morality." Andrew does not believe gay and lesbian people meet this standard of morality; again, the acceptance and welcoming of gay and lesbian people into evangelical Protestant churches are conditional.

Another way interviewees placed conditions on their acceptance of gay and lesbian people into their congregations was by placing restrictions on their behaviors. Some respondents explained that gay and lesbian people should be allowed to attend their church as long as they are not, as one respondent put it, "flaunting [their sexuality] in your face." One Catholic respondent, Brenda, said gay and lesbian people are welcome to attend church "as long as they're not trying to convert the church or change the fundamental values of our church with their beliefs." Four of the eleven Catholics interviewed described a conditional welcoming of gay and lesbian people, while only one mainline Protestant—Paula, a sixty-six-year-old white woman from the Gulf Coast of Mississippi—agreed. Paula declared that gay and lesbian people should be allowed to attend church "as long as they didn't flaunt their homosexuality, just like I don't want someone to flaunt their alcoholism. . . . I don't want that sort of thing flaunted as the accepted way to live because I don't really think it is."

As opposed to evangelical Protestants welcoming gay and lesbian people in order to change them and Catholics conditionally welcoming gay and lesbian people as long as they do not display signs of their sexuality, the majority of mainline Protestants (fifteen of nineteen) indicated gay and lesbian people should be fully welcomed into their churches without condition. These mainline Protestants and some Catholics who called for full acceptance of gay and lesbian people—either because they did not believe homosexuality is sinful or because they did not feel it is their place to make that determination—acknowledged that they are probably in the minority among Christians in Mississippi. Jason, a fifty-five-year-old white mainline Protestant pastor in central Mississippi, explained, "I would vote to ordain United Methodist clergy who are lesbian or gay. I'm probably in the minority here in Mississippi, but I would vote for it."

Beliefs diverged even further on the issue of whether gay and lesbian people should hold leadership positions in Christian churches. All evangelical Protestant respondents explained that gay and lesbian people should not be allowed to hold leadership positions in a church because they are choosing to continue living a "lifestyle" of sin. Caleb, a twenty-six-year-old white evangelical Protestant in central Mississippi, explained that he objects to gay and lesbian people holding leadership positions in his church because, in his words, "I don't think that it's pertinent to a Christian lifestyle. I don't think that homosexuality is acceptable in a Christian lifestyle, so for them to hold leadership in the church would say that the leadership isn't leading a Christian lifestyle. Our leaders in our church are people that I look to . . . an ideal to be sought after." In the same way, Darlene said gay and lesbian people cannot be leaders in a church because "I think that they're living in sin and you can't live like that. How can you uphold the beliefs if you don't really believe it?"

Catholics took the middle road on this topic; four of eleven suggested that gay and lesbian people should be completely welcomed and allowed to hold leadership positions in churches. Three Catholic respondents argued gay and lesbian people should be allowed to hold all leadership positions if they take a vow of celibacy or are not acting on their desires. A few Catholics stated that gay and lesbian people should be allowed in some positions of leadership but not others; for example, gay and lesbian people should be allowed to teach Sunday school or catechism classes but not be allowed to hold positions that require ordination. Others suggested gay and lesbian people can be priests or nuns, because this requires a vow of celibacy making their sexuality irrelevant. It is here that the conditional acceptance of gay and lesbian people in the Catholic Church becomes particularly apparent.

On the other hand, some Catholics did agree with evangelical Protestants that gay and lesbian people should not be allowed to hold any leadership positions within the church. When I asked Tim, a Catholic, if gay and lesbian people should be allowed to hold leadership positions in his church, he said, "That's a question there, kind of loaded . . . I don't really know how to answer that one. To be such a simple question, it's kind of a hard question, because if you believe in gays being wrong, well then you shouldn't believe that they should hold a leadership role in the church. I mean, it's kind of a hard stand to say 'yeah that's fine' and then you believe against what they do." Tim could not justify gay and lesbian people holding leadership positions in his church because he disagreed with the way they live their lives. Although he wished to be welcoming and accepting of everyone, he could not bring himself to say that gay and lesbian people holding leadership positions would be acceptable.

When discussing why gay and lesbian people should not hold leadership positions in Christian churches, many respondents compared homosexuality to other behaviors they believed to be sinful. For instance, Candace argued against gay and lesbian people holding leadership positions by comparing homosexuality to adultery and stealing. She stated, "People look to leaders as examples, and to me that would be like putting someone who is an adulterer in a leadership position in the church or someone who was a thief, a well-known thief, in a leadership position in the church, and that wouldn't be wise." Like Caleb explained, Candace believed that leaders in a church should be people to look up to and strive to be like.

Although many interviewees used homosexuality as justification for exclusion from God's favor, most indicated homosexuality was no worse than other sins. David said he treats homosexuality like any other sin: "It's not any worse, it's not any better. God considers sin, sin." Yet these interviewees had a difficult time explaining why, if all Christians are sinners, gay and lesbian people should be excluded from leadership positions in churches. The most common answer was that gay and lesbian people are *choosing* to continue to live a "lifestyle" of sin. When I asked Caleb why gay and lesbian people should not be allowed in leadership, since all Christians are sinners, he responded, "It depends. If somebody is striving after any sin I don't think they should be in leadership . . . I think leadership should be held to a higher standard, so it's not necessarily that they're homosexual per se. I think it's that they're living a sinful lifestyle as a Christian."

Many respondents felt that being gay or lesbian is not the sin; rather, it is acting on this desire that is sinful. One Catholic respondent, Kristina, explained, "Being homosexual is not the sin—the sin is the act of acting on being homosexual." Based on this reasoning, many respondents suggested that gay and lesbian people can and should try to change their sexuality to heterosexuality or should remain celibate, especially if they wish to serve as leaders in a church. Another Catholic, Susan, a sixty-year-old white woman living in northeast Mississippi, summed up this perspective succinctly. She argued, "If you're a married person, a male-female married person—you know, in a heterosexual relationship—and you are having an affair, you're living in a state of sin. And if you continue in that state of sin, and this is my opinion and I think that's what my church teaches, then I think it disqualifies you from some leadership roles. So if that's true, then I think if a homosexual person is in a sexual relationship that would disqualify them too. But if they're in a celibate state, I don't think that disqualifies them." Hence not all gay and lesbian people should be restricted from leadership; only those who chose to continue to have same-sex relationships. Again, we see a gradation forming, with mainline Protestants encouraging full acceptance of gay and lesbian people, Catholics moving toward acceptance but continuing to place special conditions on gay and lesbian people, and evangelical Protestants allowing gay and lesbian people to attend their churches in order to change them but unwilling to grant them equal rights within their church.

I'M RIGHT, YOU'RE WRONG

During the interviews, one question that seemed to arouse increased interest was how interviewees felt about churches that held an opposing view regarding homosexuality. For instance, when I asked David how he felt about churches that do not believe homosexuality is a sin, he responded, "I think they're apostate and they've fooled themselves into a belief that is contrary to what God has said." Frances, a fifty-year-old black evangelical Protestant from the Gulf Coast, agreed: "I don't think they're following the Bible. They can't truly believe in God's words, because otherwise they'd believe that homosexuality is a sin." Overall, eight of ten evangelical Protestants argued churches that do not believe homosexuality is sinful were misinterpreting or ignoring the Bible.

Respondents who did not feel that homosexuality was sinful—or at least not a major issue for Christians to deal with—held similarly strong beliefs about churches that disagree. Six of nineteen mainline Protestants explained they take exception to churches who overemphasize the issue of homosexuality. Mainline Protestants described churches they do not agree with as making sexuality too iconic, overemphasizing the issue of sexuality, not acting Christian, being defensive, or being fearful of change. Victor, a mainline Protestant, explained, "I think churches that [preach against homosexuality] overemphasize that part of what's going on in society . . . when other social issues should be focused on, like, inequity and income and race and access to healthcare. And I think it's easy to preach against something that you perceive to be a sin that someone else seems to be doing, and not focusing on working on what your own shortcomings are, and so I have a negative view of that." Kelsey, a mainline Protestant, expanded on this: "I think that [churches that focus on homosexuality] are really getting manipulated by conservative, Republican politics. By . . . only taking a small percentage of the population and saying, 'Well they're the worst sinners' . . . why don't we talk about sins that everybody does, like greed, envy, slander—you know, all that stuff?" Previous research supports Kelsey's claim that individuals' religious beliefs are being directed toward opposition of gay and lesbian civil rights through ties with evangelical political organizations and the Republican Party (Sherkat et al. 2011). Similarly, three of eleven Catholics interviewed believed other churches are causing more problems than they are solving by focusing so heavily on sexuality. When asked about churches that focus significant attention on homosexuality, one Catholic, Tracy, a sixty-three-year-old white woman from northeast Mississippi, explained, "It saddens me because I think it boils down to attacking individuals, and it smacks of homophobia to me. . . . It's like we're on the right side and you're on the wrong side, and I don't think that's what Jesus came to talk about." Similarly, other Catholics explained that they believed these churches are being judgmental, fearful, and divisive.

Clearly, there is not a consensus among Christians on the issue of homosexuality. Both sides of this divide have fairly strong and negative opinions of the other. What this means for Christians as a whole is less clear, but we can safely say that the Mississippi Christians in this study have very different perspectives on the issue of homosexuality and how (or if) it should be addressed in their church or denomination.

*　*　*　*　*

Overall, the respondents in this study held diverse views about the Bible and homosexuality. The evangelical Protestants interviewed argued for a literal interpretation of the Bible, but this interpretation was strongly influenced by their biases, understanding of the

Bible as a document about sin and salvation, and pastors' beliefs about what the Bible says. The evangelical Protestant respondents all felt that homosexuality was sinful based on their interpretations of the Bible, whether they knew exactly where the Bible said this or not. Evangelical Protestants only wished to welcome gay and lesbian people into their church in order to change their sexuality, and they argued that gay and lesbian people should not hold leadership positions within the church.

Catholic respondents typically felt that it was their priest or the Catholic Church's responsibility to interpret scripture. Most believed that homosexuality was sinful, because this was the official stance of their individual priests or the Catholic Church. When it came to allowing gay and lesbian people into the Catholic Church, the Mississippi Catholics in this study offered conditional acceptance; they believed that gay and lesbian people should be welcomed into the church as long as they kept their sexuality quiet and did not try to change the church's teachings.

Finally, the mainline Protestants interviewed for this project offered a more complete acceptance of gay and lesbian people into their churches. Most mainline Protestants interpreted the Bible through a lens of love and nonjudgment. This hermeneutic circle led them to ignore or interpret the passages used to condemn homosexuality differently than evangelical Protestants. Generally, mainline Protestants argued it was not their place to judge and that they believed gay and lesbian people should be allowed to hold leadership positions within their churches.

Evangelical Protestants were, by and large, the most conservative of Mississippi Christians and sought to set themselves apart from society by showing that Christians are—or at least should be—different from others. One evangelical Protestant, Caleb, clearly articulated the importance of Christians setting themselves apart and refusing to compromise when it comes to their beliefs. He said, "To not acknowledge what the Bible says is to lie to God and lie to yourself. . . . This may sound terrible, but I think that a lot of churches are so worried about not offending someone . . . and they're so worried about how many people are in attendance

and showing them love, but that's not true love I don't think. . . .
There shouldn't be compromise in the gospel; there shouldn't be
compromise in the beliefs of God. But there also shouldn't
be compromise in the way that we approach people with love."
Caleb unmistakably believed that Christians should not and cannot compromise when it comes to the teachings of the Bible. He
believed that Christians have sacrificed too much in the name of
"political correctness"and that evangelical Protestants must go back
to the Bible in order to set themselves apart from secular society.
These findings support Smith et al.'s (1998) thesis of subcultural
identity theory. Evangelical Protestant interviewees' beliefs about
what the Bible and their church say about homosexuality continue
to support an embattled identity that separates them from the rest
of society. As Smith et al. (1998) explain, this allows evangelical
Protestants to thrive as a religion, because the distinction they feel
gives them an important identity marker.

Conversely, beliefs about homosexuality are another way mainline Protestants continue to move toward assimilation with secular
society. Many mainline Protestants interviewed felt the Bible said
nothing about homosexuality and that Christians must fully accept
gay and lesbian people into their churches. In Mississippi, the
beliefs of the Catholics I interviewed appeared to fall somewhere
between evangelical and mainline Protestants. Overall, Catholics
showed more uncertainty about the issue of homosexuality; they
were neither fully in agreement with larger societal views, nor did
they appear to be embattled by it. This middle ground may be
why Catholics' answers appear more ambivalent or uncertain. This
ambivalence and uncertainty becomes even more evident when
discussing opinions about gay and lesbian rights; this is the task of
the next section of this book.

PART 2

Gay and Lesbian Civil Rights

3

Marriage = 1 Man + 1 Woman?

Support and Opposition to Same-Sex Marriage

> God is not going to allow the sin to continue like it's going, and if our
> country votes to let gay or lesbian people be able to get married and all
> this mess, then it's just another slap in God's face, and, I mean, he's going
> to put his hand down and say, "Enough is enough, and you've turned your
> back on me enough," and he will call those home who have accepted
> him, and he will let the others go where they have chosen to go.... I feel
> that things that happen to this nation—like earthquakes and hurricanes
> and all of that kind of stuff—I feel like God allows those things to happen,
> because he's trying to get our attention ... just like how Katrina hit New
> Orleans and almost wiped it out. You know, God was trying to get the
> people in New Orleans' attention and the people down on the coast.
>
> —Angela, a fifty-three-year-old white evangelical
> Protestant from the Gulf Coast

Understanding how Christians view gay and lesbian civil rights is
critically important in the United States, especially in the Southeast. Discrimination and denial of equal rights for any group leads
to serious societal consequences, including unequal social structures and policies that continue to perpetuate sexual stigma and
prejudice (Goffman 1963; Herek 2011). According to the Human
Rights Campaign (Peters 2016), more than 115 anti-LGBT bills
were introduced in 2015 alone. Historically, groups in opposition

to gay and lesbian equality have had disproportionate success in passing legislation in the United States (McVeigh and Diaz 2009). Those who desire to limit the opportunities of gay and lesbian people continue to hold power and influence in this country.

Specifically, in Mississippi, HB 1523—the "religious freedom" bill discussed in the introduction—was supported by politically and religiously conservative groups in order to legally deny rights to gay and lesbian citizens. Not surprisingly, negative beliefs and attitudes toward homosexuality have been proven to be dependable predictors of voting behaviors surrounding gay and lesbian policies (Herek 2000; Saucier and Cawman 2004). Beliefs and attitudes about gay and lesbian civil rights are more than personal opinions; these largely religious beliefs continue to guide legislation and the life circumstances of gay and lesbian people.

Allowing gay and lesbian rights to be stifled by conservative Christians is obviously detrimental to gay and lesbian individuals, as sexual stigma continues to lead to oppression and disempowerment (Herek 2011). In order to change legislation and ensure gay and lesbian people equal treatment under the law, it is imperative to understand why many Christians continue to hold negative attitudes about homosexuality and vote against equality for gay and lesbian people. Overcoming sexual stigma and empowering gay and lesbian people are first steps in reducing the societal consequences of homophobia and heterosexism. This is a vital project because individuals who are stigmatized due to their sexual orientation have less access to resources (jobs, housing, education, etc.) and less control over their own lives (Herek 2011).

Why Do Conservative Christians Oppose Gay and Lesbian Equality?

Preconceived notions of religion as unchangeable and always salient have led many scholars to stop short of fully understanding why Christians continue to hold significant prejudice toward gay and lesbian people. Biblical passages are quoted as justification for opposition to homosexuality, but few have examined how these passages lead conservative Christians to oppose gay and lesbian rights. Taking Biblical literalism as a complete justification for opposition to homosexuality and gay and lesbian rights has halted further investigation into the justification of conservative Christians' arguments. Accepting this single explanation provides only a partial understanding of opposition to gay and lesbian equality.

Conservative Christians' accounts of their religious beliefs and how these relate to gay and lesbian civil rights show a more complex view of homosexuality than previous research indicates. Conservative Christians' nuanced understandings and explanations of how they overcome the inconsistencies between their personal relationships with gay and lesbian people and their conservative religious beliefs about homosexuality reveal a much more in-depth thought process than merely acceptance or rejection. By examining this topic more carefully, I argue it is not "hate"— hostility or intolerance toward gay and lesbian people—per se that drives many Christians to oppose gay and lesbian civil rights or homosexuality more generally. Rather, it is conservative Christians' sincere religious convictions that lead them to believe the only way to help gay and lesbian people is by supporting them in changing or denying their sexuality. Because of these strong religious beliefs, knowing someone who identifies as gay or lesbian, which often leads less religiously conservative Americans to shift toward more positive beliefs and attitudes about gay and lesbian people, does not produce the same positive influence among conservative Christians.

Certainly, there are still some conservative Christians driven to oppose gay and lesbian rights due to homophobia and hatred, but that was not the case for most respondents in this study. In fact, the majority of respondents who opposed gay and lesbian rights in this study argued they do so from a place of love and compassion. Because many conservative Christians truly felt that homosexuality was sinful and harmful to both the individual and society, they believed it was their Christian duty to help gay and lesbian people overcome this "sin." While homophobia is based on aversion to and prejudice against lesbian and gay people and often leads to discrimination and oppression, the conservative Christians in this study argued these were not their feelings. They distinguished between disliking gay and lesbian people and worrying about the sinful nature of homosexual acts. The fact that some conservative Christians in this study had friends who were "ex-gay" was used to demonstrate that their beliefs and feelings were a hatred not of people but rather of sinful behaviors.

Many interviewees demonstrated sympathy for gay and lesbian people but were unable to fully empathize with this group. This distinction may seem trivial, but the difference in emotions between sympathy and empathy is significant. Sympathy suggests a person feels compassion or pity for someone else's suffering or difficulties. Empathy, on the other hand, implies the deeper emotion of being able to actually feel another person's pain or suffering. As the saying goes, empathy is the ability to "put yourself in someone else's shoes." While some respondents were able to feel sympathy for gay and lesbian people, due to their conservative religious beliefs, few were able to fully understand the pain and suffering resulting from unequal rights for gay and lesbian citizens. While these respondents certainly did not hate gay and lesbian individuals, they were unable to empathize with their societal plight. This inability to empathize with gay and lesbian people seems primarily due to conservative Christians' fears concerning gay and lesbian equality. These fears range from misunderstandings of the impacts of same-sex marriage and adoption on children to extreme beliefs that gay and lesbian equality could bring the world as we know it to an end.

At this important time in American history as gay and lesbian civil rights have taken center stage, it is critical to understand those who continue to oppose rights for gay and lesbian people. In order for advocates of equality to bring about change, it is helpful to understand the beliefs and attitudes of their opposition, especially since those who oppose equal rights for gay and lesbian people have seen great success politically. Because conservative Christians take a lead role in speaking out against equal rights for gay and lesbian individuals (Fetner 2008), it is essential to consider what factors are effective in decreasing inaccurate beliefs and negative attitudes toward gay and lesbian people within the Christian community. While other discriminatory belief systems such as racism, classism, and nativism seem to be based in broader ideological structures, homophobia and heterosexism continue to revolve around conservative religious ideology. Therefore, it is imperative to understand the beliefs of Christians in the United States in order to overcome homophobia and heterosexism.

Additionally, the ambivalence and contradictions that appear to be inherent within religion indicate a need to dig deeper to understand a person's beliefs about morality and social issues. Simply relying on what religious leaders say or a single interpretation of the Bible is not sufficient to know the stance any individual Christian will take on an issue. To heed the advice of Smith (2000) and others, to truly understand Christians' beliefs and practices we have to talk to them and observe them. A goal of this study is to listen to Mississippi Christians' beliefs about gay and lesbian rights in order to examine why Christianity continues to be a driving force behind social structures and policies that limit the life choices of gay and lesbian people in the United States. While there are many rights for gay and lesbian people that remain contested, this study specifically focuses on the rights of same-sex marriage (chapter 3), adoption (chapter 4), and the larger gay and lesbian civil rights movement (chapter 5). Although the respondents in this study had divided opinions regarding these specific rights, they generally agreed that the gay and lesbian civil rights movement signifies a decline in morality in the United States.

The period of time over which interviews were conducted—between September and December of 2013—is particularly significant for discussing the issue of same-sex marriage in the United States for a number of reasons. First, these interviews were conducted approximately a decade after same-sex marriage became a nationwide debate in the United States. In 2003, the attitudinal shift toward acceptance of gay and lesbian civil rights became obvious when the Supreme Judicial Court of Massachusetts ruled in *Goodridge et al. v. Department of Public Health* that only marriage could provide same-sex couples with equality. This decision meant same-sex couples in Massachusetts could begin legally marrying in May 2004 (Simon 2013).

For the first time in 2010, and again in 2011, a CNN (2010) poll and separate Gallup poll (Newport 2011) recorded that a slight majority of Americans were in favor of legalizing same-sex marriage. On June 26, 2013, less than three months before I began interviews for this project, the U.S. Supreme Court ruled in *Windsor v. United States* that a key part of the Defense of Marriage Act (DOMA) was unconstitutional, a ruling that ensured federal marriage benefits for legally married same-sex couples across the United States (Freedom to Marry 2018b). However, it was not until almost two years after these data were collected, in June 2015, that the U.S. Supreme Court ruled to guarantee same-sex couples the right to marry in all states in *Obergefell v. Hodges*. Therefore, while same-sex couples could marry in another state and be recognized in Mississippi, the right of same-sex couples to actually *get* married in the state of Mississippi was still a hypothetical notion at the time I spoke with the Christians in this study. With this context in mind, we can better appreciate the attitudes and beliefs respondents held concerning same-sex marriage.

Mississippi Christians' Beliefs about Same-Sex Marriage

Overall, interviewees held strong beliefs and attitudes about the issue of same-sex marriage. In general, the respondents in this study reflected higher rates of opposition to same-sex marriage than other Americans. The country began to tip in favor of marriage equality in 2010, and by 2014, approximately 55 percent of Americans believed same-sex marriages should be recognized as valid and granted the same rights as "traditional marriages." This support rose to an all-time high of 67 percent in 2018 (Gallup 2018). The respondents in this study revealed equal support and opposition to same-sex marriage, however, and the stories behind these numbers are complicated.

In total, nine of the forty respondents were completely opposed to recognizing same-sex marriage, including civil unions. This includes six of ten evangelical Protestants, two of eleven Catholics, and one of nineteen mainline Protestants. These respondents represented the image of conservative Mississippi that the media has painted so well. Based almost completely on religious ideology, these respondents felt that gay and lesbian individuals do not deserve the right to marry whom they wish. They expressed fear that equality for gays and lesbians would be harmful to others, especially Christians.

Eleven out of forty interviewees argued that even if same-sex couples were granted equal rights, these rights should not include marriage. Many of these respondents supported the "separate but equal" idea of civil unions or something comparable. The majority of Catholics (six of eleven) argued for "equality" but not marriage, along with three mainline Protestants and two evangelical Protestants. Here again, the fear was obvious about the broader consequences of same-sex marriage, but the fear of these respondents was more focused on children, the family, and religious beliefs rather than the end of the world. The main theme for these respondents was that marriage is a religious institution. While those who argued for a "not marriage" alternative wanted gay and lesbian individuals to be equal as citizens, they did not believe that gay and lesbian individuals should be granted access to the religious institution of marriage. They felt that same-sex marriage devalued the religious aspect and meaning of the marriage covenant but simultaneously wanted to be open-minded and accepting.

Finally, twenty interviewees said they supported same-sex marriage. While the majority of mainline Protestants fell into this group (fifteen of nineteen), only three Catholics and two evangelical Protestants supported same-sex marriage. Importantly, the two evangelical Protestants who stated they supported same-sex marriage made it extremely clear that this was only because they viewed marriage as a meaningless institution and felt that the government did not have a right to control this aspect of peoples' lives.

When it came to marriage as a religious institution, both evangelical respondents were completely opposed to allowing gay and lesbian people to partake in this ceremony of the church. On the other hand, the mainline Protestants and more liberal Catholics felt that gay and lesbian individuals had the right to be married and did not qualify their answers. To examine how respondents justified their responses to same-sex marriage, I consider the three different categories of responses in turn: complete opposition to same-sex marriage, including civil unions; support of equality, but not marriage; and full support of same-sex marriage.

THE END OF THE WORLD AS WE KNOW IT: CONSERVATIVE CHRISTIANS' OPPOSITION TO SAME-SEX MARRIAGE

Evangelical Protestants interviewed displayed their fears clearly when discussing the issue of same-sex marriage. They generally believed that same-sex marriage was the beginning of the "downward spiral" of society. This panic was based on a concrete belief that the foundation of society is the "traditional" family. The belief that the 1950s (white, middle-class) version of family is the only true type of family runs deep in this community. Evangelical Protestants in Mississippi held tight to the *Leave It to Beaver* version of family with a husband (man/breadwinner), wife (woman/housekeeper), and two kids living the perfect suburban life. Although this type of family was never actually the norm (Coontz 1992), they have romanticized this configuration and deemed it the "Christian family."

This dedication to a specific type of family is also related to evangelical Protestants' subcultural identity. Feeling that their idea of family, which is wrapped up with their beliefs about gender and sexuality, is being challenged, evangelical Protestants feel they must protect the boundaries of their faith from the encroaching secular world. Thus embattled by the forces of evil, including homosexuality, evangelical Christians continue to draw a line in the sand when it comes to gay and lesbian rights.

Based on this belief of the nuclear family as the foundation of a stable and godly world, the majority of Mississippi evangelical

Protestants in this study expressed total opposition to same-sex marriage. In fact, only two evangelical Protestant interviewees believed that civil marriage was a right same-sex couples should be entitled to, and no evangelicals felt that marriage in the church was appropriate for same-sex couples.[1] Only two Catholics and one mainline Protestant agreed that same-sex marriage was a threat to the family as the foundation of society. In addition to same-sex marriage threatening the family structure and society at large, the respondents who were opposed to same-sex marriage, including civil unions, generally understood marriage as a religious institution. Most often these respondents believed that homosexuality is sinful and goes against the teachings of the Bible. These respondents also suggested that a broadening of the definition of marriage to include same-sex couples would inevitably open a door and allow other groups to fight for the right to marry. In the extreme form, same-sex marriage was compared to the desire to marry animals. Others equated the fight for same-sex marriage with the fight for the legalization of polygamy. One evangelical respondent, Andrew, summed up opposition to same-sex marriage this way: "In other societies, there have been homosexual and lesbian relationships, but it's never been called marriage. I think to redefine basic human relationships is different than letting people have relationships that they want, but to redefine marriage, I think is a problem. . . . You're losing the foundation of society . . . weakening the foundation of a community." From Andrew's perspective, society is based on the foundation of the heterosexual family. He believed that while people may form other relationships that depart from this foundation, we cannot allow these relationships the same recognition as the relationship between a heterosexual couple.

In line with Angela (quoted at the beginning of the chapter), Erica, another evangelical Protestant, held an extreme view of same-sex marriage. She argued that same-sex marriage would not only weaken the foundation of society and community but also lead to the eventual destruction of the world as we know it. She explained that same-sex marriage is "just another way that the nation is going against God's will, and it leads to death." Not only did same-sex marriage go against her traditional understanding of family and her religious beliefs, but it also directly defied the will of God. She felt that the consequences for such a transgression against God would only be death. Erica was referring not just to the death of same-sex couples but also to the ultimate death of all people for allowing such disobedience to occur in their presence. When asked if she would support same-sex civil unions instead of marriage, she responded, "I couldn't . . . because then taxpayers' money and all of those things would be going against what God says." In Erica's eyes, any ounce of support for same-sex couples' rights defied God and would be harmful to society and everyone in it. This apocalyptic view clearly meant that there were no compromises to be made; it was, by definition, a life-or-death matter for Erica.

Another evangelical Protestant, Candace, also expressed grave fear, but her fear was for the safety of herself and other evangelical Protestants who disagreed with same-sex marriage. When I asked her if she supported same-sex marriage, she explained:

> It's a tricky question, because if you say yes, it's almost like the group that is pushing to have [same-sex marriage] legalized in our nation is not satisfied with that, and so it's just like one step down a pathway that is basically, in my view, going to lead to the fact that they don't want pastors to be able to speak the truth from the pulpit. . . . I'm talking about the activists now. They're the ones putting pressure on our government leaders and people making decisions that are going to possibly end up meaning that I'm going to go to jail eventually. Because if I felt that it was important to speak the truth to someone walking in that lifestyle, and then I got turned in, then I would go to jail. In other words, we're talking about a long pathway here, and I mean we went from a point in the United States where every state had a sodomy law and homosexuality was illegal, now to a place where homosexuality is not made a big deal of at all. . . . They're trying to have homosexuality a protected group which makes them even more protected than anyone else. . . . I think that's one more step

down this pathway to homosexuals demanding that the lifestyle not only be accepted but actually be promoted.

Clearly, Candace was extremely upset with activists for gay and lesbian rights; she believed that providing equal rights to gay and lesbian people meant they would be more protected than heterosexual people. Her fear of ending up in jail because of her beliefs was palpable. To some, this response may sound ridiculous and more like fearmongering than true belief, but to Candace, it was real. Candace believed that allowing same-sex couples to marry would end only in the government encouraging all people to become gay or lesbian and the "promotion" of homosexuality.

While most Catholics interviewed took more of a middle-of-the-road stance on same-sex marriage, two Catholic interviewees agreed with evangelical Protestants that same-sex marriage should not be allowed in the United States under any circumstances. For example, Kristina's answer on the question of same-sex marriage mirrored evangelical Protestants' answers. When asked if gay and lesbian people should be allowed to marry, she said no, explaining,

> In God's aspect, and the religious aspect of it, that's just one more way that we are falling away from God and falling away from the morality that he set forth for us to function [not only] in a worshipping community but as a functioning society. You know, first it's OK to marry the same sex. Second, it's OK to, I don't know, do the purge day [one day a year you can commit any crime that you want to]. . . . You know, I just think that it opens a gateway into making anything and everything that we want to do OK, and that's just not what God wants for us.

Most Catholics did not describe same-sex marriage in this condemning way; Kristina's fear of the negative influences of same-sex marriage fell outside the realm of possibility for the majority of other Mississippi Catholics.

As mentioned, even though most evangelical respondents agreed that same-sex marriage should be strongly opposed, two evangelical respondents did indicate a form of support for same-sex marriage. I discuss these respondents separately rather than with those who support same-sex marriage, because they continued to hold that homosexuality is sinful and should not be allowed. The only reason these two evangelical Protestants supported same-sex marriage was because they felt that marriage in our society was no longer sacred—religious or related to God—and that the state has no right to control an individual's choices. Caleb explained, "My marriage—the promise that I made to my wife, the covenant that I made before God—really has nothing to do with [the] American government. That's just a tax rate write-off. So yeah, I see no problem with homosexuals being allowed to get married in America." Noticeably, he did not support same-sex marriage because he believed it is morally just or in line with his religious beliefs; rather, Caleb and the other evangelical Protestant who supported same-sex marriage did so because they believed marriage was no longer a religious institution and did not feel that allowing same-sex marriage would be detrimental to their own lives. Caleb clearly separated the political institution of marriage from the "covenant he made before God." He made clear that he believes homosexuality is sinful and goes against the teachings of the Bible, but his strong belief in minimizing the government's power over individuals led to a position that may seem contradictory at first glance. This opinion is based on libertarian political views rather than religious convictions.

Only one mainline Protestant, Brad, felt that same-sex marriage was not morally reprehensible but was still completely opposed. He explained that it was not Christians' place to judge others, and he did not feel that homosexuality was sinful. Yet when I asked Brad if same-sex couples should be allowed to marry, he responded:

I don't think so. . . . I think that's just kind of a personal thing. I don't really have any justified basis to it. You know, I guess in my upbringing. Although it's acceptable, I just don't feel that it's right. . . . I think the divorce rate would go up still . . . because I don't think homosexual couples are any different than heterosexual couples. . . . I think a lot of [same-sex couples] still go into marriage with the intention that it's not forever, you know, we can get out of this if need be. And I would think that maybe two women together, or two men together, may not get along as well as, you know, a man and a woman.

Although it does appear that Brad had some preconceived notions about gender and what makes a marriage that seemed to be based in religion, he still argued that religious organizations do not have the right to discriminate against gay and lesbian people. At the same time, Brad clearly had hesitations about allowing same-sex couples the same rights as heterosexual couples.

JUST DON'T CALL IT MARRIAGE: SUPPORT FOR CIVIL UNIONS, BUT NOT MARRIAGE

The respondents in this category believed that gay and lesbian people deserve legal protections and benefits but would not call it "marriage." They were more likely to support civil unions or piece-meal granting of smaller rights inherent to marriage in the United States. Christians in this group typically felt that homosexuality was not ideal or what God intended, but at the same time, they wished to be fair. There was also a clear division in their answers between marriage as a religious institution and marriage as a civil institution. There was a desire to reserve the term "marriage" for the church and refer to the civil institution of marriage with different terminology.

Six of the eleven Catholics interviewed believed that gay and lesbian people deserved equality but were clear that these rights should not be deemed marriage. In addition to these Catholics, two evangelical Protestants and three mainline Protestants indicated support for civil unions but not marriage. As a general trend in this study, Catholics seemed to hold more ambivalent views about gay and lesbian rights than Protestants. This middle ground allowed Mississippi Catholics to simultaneously denounce same-sex marriage in the church while supporting some or all of the civil rights marriage guarantees in the United States. The ideas about "traditional" family and marriage for the purpose of procreation crept back into the conversation for this group of respondents.

Brenda, a Catholic, exemplified this sentiment; she felt gay and lesbian people should be free to love whom they choose and should have the same rights when it comes to economic benefits. She also believed, however, that the institution of marriage was meant for heterosexual couples for the purpose of procreation only. When asked if same-sex couples should have the right to marry, Brenda explained:

> I struggle with that. I think that there should be some inherent rights preserved for traditional family. . . . I can't say I'm opposed to marriage, but I think—again, going back to Christianity and maybe the Bible—that marriage is something that should be reserved for husband and wife for the sake of having children, biological children . . . [gay and lesbian people] can do what they do, but—you know, being that I'm a taxpayer and supportive of all the insurance things—you know I think marriage still probably, as an institution, should be reserved for heterosexual couples for the true purpose of having biological children.

To Brenda, marriage between people of the opposite sex was in some way superior to same-sex marriage, and the ability to reproduce children biologically inherently imbued heterosexual couples with rights that should not be extended to other types of families.

Another Catholic, Phillip, also felt that marriage should be reserved for heterosexual couples and reiterated the point about procreation. While he believed that same-sex couples should be allowed to have the rights granted through marriage, he believed that calling same-sex partnerships "marriage" took it a step too far:

To me, marriage is a very specific thing, and I don't think marriage—as I believe in marriage and understand marriage— I don't think that applies to people of the same sex. So, I believe that [same-sex couples] should be allowed to form civil unions, which is a word that I've read a lot in recent history that I think I somewhat understand and agree with. They're free to choose the way they want to live, any way they want to live. But to elevate that union to the same level as a covenantal relationship in marriage, I don't think they're the same thing. There really is a difference, but they're free to live however they choose.

Here, Phillip used terminology very similar to evangelical Protestant Caleb; however, to Phillip, "a covenantal relationship" was the same as marriage and therefore reserved for heterosexual couples. Phillip went on to discuss procreation as a requirement of the true meaning of marriage. I followed up by asking him if he believed heterosexual couples that are infertile or choose not to have children should be allowed to marry. His answer demonstrated the complexity surrounding many Catholics' justification for limiting gay and lesbian rights. He explained, "That's true, [some heterosexual couples cannot or do not want to have children], but the purpose, whether or not that purpose is fulfilled, doesn't change the description of what [marriage] is. . . . Listen, I'm seventy-one, I can't have kids anymore. I remarried after [my spouse] died. I met a wonderful lady; we fell in love and married just recently. So, I can't have kids; neither can she. But we're still sexually active. You know, because that's the secondary part, but the purpose of that union still exists, even though it may not be fulfilled." According to Phillip, opposite-sex couples that cannot or choose not to have children can still enter into "marriages" because the ability to reproduce *could* have existed.

The insistence that same-sex marriage should not be allowed but that same-sex couples deserve some form of legal recognition seemed to be directly tied to Catholics' belief in marriage as one of the seven sacraments—religious acts showing your devotion and relationship with God—in the Catholic Church. Susan most clearly articulated this point. She explained, "I think that there could be civil laws that would cover any kind of civil union. I just feel like marriage is a sacrament, and I know that's getting religion mixed up in politics and public life and all, but I just feel like for centuries marriage has been a sacrament, and it's been understood that way and it should stay that way. But I don't think that there's any reason why we can't have civil union laws that would, you know, meet the requirements that homosexuals would need for legal status." While Susan believed that gay and lesbian people should have equal legal status, she did not believe that these relationships should be blessed as a symbol of their devotion to God. Susan was unable to separate the meaning of marriage from her religious beliefs; therefore, she advocated for civil unions in place of marriage for same-sex couples.

Unlike other Catholic and evangelical Protestant respondents, Wendy, a fifty-three-year-old mainline Protestant from the Gulf Coast of Mississippi, believed that same-sex unions can be a religious act, although she still felt they have to be separated from "traditional marriage." She explained, "I believe that there should be some way for people who are committed to each other to be protected by laws. I don't know that I believe that it should be a traditional marriage ceremony. But I do believe that if two people want to be committed in the eyes of God to each other, then there should be some kind of symbol, something. Yeah, that's what I believe. . . . I don't personally believe that there should be a traditional marriage." Wendy did not feel the symbolic, religious meaning of marriage should be denied to same-sex couples, but she fell short of recognizing same-sex unions as equivalent to heterosexual unions.

Overall, those in the category supporting civil unions rather than marriage stressed the "traditional" and religious aspects of marriage. These interviewees could not condone admittance to a historically heterosexual institution, even if they did feel that gay and lesbian people deserved to live in a just society. Although they were not sure what they would lose, it appeared that allowing gay and lesbian couples the right to marry would in some way devalue the institution of marriage between opposite-sex couples.

"DO NOT JUDGE, OR YOU TOO WILL BE JUDGED"[2]: SUPPORT FOR SAME-SEX MARRIAGE

In contrast to those who opposed same-sex marriage, some Christians in this study believed that supporting same-sex marriage was in line with their religious principles or that it at least did not contradict those principles. Those who supported same-sex marriage generally did not believe that homosexuality was innately sinful. Many pointed to biblical passages that encouraged Christians not to pass judgment on one another and to love one another. These Christians also felt that allowing gay and lesbian people to marry would have positive benefits for the country more generally. Overall, respondents who supported same-sex marriage felt that providing gay and lesbian people the opportunity to marry would actually strengthen the family unit, not break it down. Those who fully supported same-sex marriage typically identified as mainline Protestants; in fact, only one mainline Protestant indicated total opposition to same-sex marriage. In addition to the fifteen mainline Protestants, three Catholics also supported same-sex marriage.

Instead of focusing on the harm same-sex marriage could cause to society, mainline Protestants focused on the benefits of allowing gay and lesbian people the right to marry. As one respondent, Jason, explained, same-sex marriage would bring about positive change in this country, especially when it comes to "taxes and equality." Along the same lines, Victor agreed same-sex marriage would lead to "significant economic benefits." He continued, "And I think, within a few years, it will be much more accepted than it's now, just like interracial marriage was a generation or two ago . . . but now not many people think very much about it." According to these respondents, if people had time to get used to it, society could benefit from allowing same-sex couples to marry.

While Jason and Victor pointed to the economic benefits of same-sex marriage, Kelsey saw more ideological benefits. She stated, "I do think [same-sex marriage] might promote marriage. I think it might strengthen people's opinion of actually getting married. . . . I feel like people are realizing it's not really that big of a deal." Unlike some evangelical Protestants and Catholics who argued that same-sex marriage was acceptable because the meaning of marriage has changed or diminished, Kelsey believed that same-sex marriage could actually strengthen the institution of marriage. By allowing people to marry whomever they wished rather than those whom they were "supposed" to marry by society's standards, Kelsey assumed people would be happier and have healthier marriages. Like Victor, she also believed that, given time, people would forget about this issue and move on to something new.

A final justification for support of same-sex marriage was the impact it would have on children. Some mainline Protestants explained that they supported same-sex marriage because it would make it easier for gay and lesbian people to adopt children. Additionally, legal recognition of marriage would mean that same-sex couples would have the same rights as heterosexual couples when it came to their children. Same-sex marriage would make life easier not only for parents but also for their children. Casey, a mainline Protestant, put it this way: "I don't see negative consequences [of same-sex marriage] in terms of family stability, in terms of financial consequences, anything like that. I think allowing people to be who they are, and love who they love, is the most important thing. . . . Maybe people in same-sex marriages might be better able to adopt children . . . if their marriage was legalized. . . . As for the child and negative impacts, I don't feel that there would be any." Rick, a Catholic, agreed with Casey, saying, "I think [same-sex marriage] is a good thing. . . . I think it would allow children who have gay parents to feel normal." Both Casey and Rick believed there are many children in the United States who need good homes and that same-sex couples can provide them this stability. Both understood that allowing same-sex couples equal rights would make life better for the children in these homes. As Rick articulated, normalizing same-sex families would remove some of the stigma for the parents as well as for the children.

Those respondents who supported same-sex marriage did not feel threatened by allowing gay and lesbian couples equal rights. In fact, the majority of these respondents believed that same-sex marriage would have only positive effects on society, including economic and ideological benefits as well as advantages for family stability. In opposition to those who feared the downfall of society or the "traditional" family, these respondents believed that equality makes a stronger and better society. Most importantly, they felt that supporting gay and lesbian people's right to marry did not contradict their religious beliefs, and moreover, many felt this was the Christian position to take on the issue of same-sex marriage. These interviewees interpreted the Bible in a way that was accepting of gay and lesbian people. They did not feel a need to choose between Christianity and accepting gay and lesbian friends and family members. This group of respondents challenged the one-sided and narrow view society paints of the Deep South. They demonstrated how religious beliefs in the South can be open-minded and supportive of equality. Their responses indicate there is hope for reconciling religion and sexuality, even in the most conservative area of the country. These respondents illustrate that viewing the South through a single lens ignores the complex reality of what is truly happening there.

*   *   *   *   *

As the issue of same-sex marriage illustrates, Mississippi Christians' beliefs about gay and lesbian civil rights are highly variable and ambivalent. Many of the responses seem contradictory when it comes to which rights should be granted to gay and lesbian people. While understanding beliefs and attitudes about same-sex marriage seems to explain a broader story about gay and lesbian rights, Mississippi Christians' belief systems are not always predictable, and on the surface, many times their views do not appear to line up in a logical way. Based on an understanding of respondents' beliefs about same-sex marriage, it would make sense that we could now accurately predict their stances on the issue of same-sex adoption. Alas, with ambiguity and a complex system of beliefs, respondents justify positions that do not always appear to align. In the next chapter, I consider how Mississippi Christians make sense of the issue of same-sex adoption.

4

Do Children Need a Mom and a Dad?

The Debate over Same-Sex Adoption

I don't have a problem with [same-sex adoption] really, especially given
all the kids that need good homes ... as long as they don't try to push
their homosexual values on them. We're all inherently heterosexual,
so they say. ... If I was a homosexual couple and I adopted what
would seem to be a heterosexual child, I wouldn't try to make that
child homosexual. ... And I would also hope if it was a male or female
couple they would try to bring other outside influences, other family
members, whoever, so that the child, if it was a male child [and] had
two moms, could be exposed to the male, you know, genre.
—Brenda, a forty-four-year-old white Catholic from the Gulf Coast

The issue of same-sex adoption appeared to be even more complex
than marriage for the respondents in this study. Many respondents believed gay and lesbian people should not be allowed to
adopt children, but their answers also illustrated the ambiguity
and confusion they felt about this topic. Several interviewees who
were opposed to same-sex marriage either fully or conditionally
supported same-sex adoption. These respondents were able to fit
these apparent discrepancies into a coherent ideological belief system. Similar to their opinions on same-sex marriage, respondents'
beliefs about same-sex adoption fell along a continuum of support clearly mediated by religious affiliation: mainline Protestants

offered the most support for same-sex adoption, evangelical Protestants were opposed to same-sex adoption, and Catholics landed in-between, with complicated answers and beliefs about the best way to merge their faith with the reality of our current society.

The issue of same-sex adoption is especially pertinent in the state of Mississippi for a number of reasons. Mississippi was the last state in the country to continue upholding legislation that blocked same-sex couples from adopting. At the time the data for this project were collected, same-sex adoption was still illegal in the state. In fact, it was not until March 31, 2016, that a federal judge ruled that Mississippi's ban on same-sex adoption was unconstitutional (Karimi 2016). The issue of same-sex adoption in Mississippi is also important because, according to the 2010 U.S. Census, Mississippi was the state with the highest proportion (26 percent) of same-sex couples raising children in the United States (Gates 2013). Finally, it is possible that adoption agencies can again turn away same-sex couples under the new Religious Liberty Accommodations Act (HB 1523) that went into effect on October 10, 2017. By citing personal religious beliefs, workers at both private and state-funded adoption agencies can now legally turn away same-sex couples. Therefore, it is critical to understand what Christians believe about the issue of same-sex adoption. To do so, I will discuss the various stances respondents had on the issue of same-sex adoption, starting first with those who felt that same-sex adoption should be illegal and is detrimental to children. I will then follow with a discussion of respondents who believed same-sex adoption is not ideal but is a better option than leaving children in a failing foster care system. Finally, I will discuss those interviewees who were supportive of same-sex adoption.

Hide the Kids: A Case for "Traditional" Family

The respondents who were completely opposed to gay and lesbian people having the right to adopt children in the United States felt that same-sex adoption would harm children. Some argued that children raised by same-sex parents would be more likely to grow up and identify as gay or lesbian. Overall, nine interviewees (one mainline Protestant and eight evangelical Protestants) held this exclusionary position on same-sex adoption. The bulk of their arguments were based on ideas of "traditional" family and gender essentialism. These interviewees believed that for a child to be successful they need both a mother (who is a woman) and a father (who is a man). This is especially interesting in a state where almost half of children are being raised in single-parent families. In 2012, 35 percent of children in the United States were being raised in single-parent families, compared to 49 percent in Mississippi (Annie E. Casey Foundation 2014).

Despite the fact that the majority of children in Mississippi are not being raised in a "traditional," nuclear family, this model was still the gold standard and measure of family to most evangelical Protestants in this study. While family was a centerpiece of evangelicals' beliefs, they were not willing to open it to other iterations. Evangelical Protestants argued that gay and lesbian people were trying to reap the benefits of a system that they refused to buy into—that is, heterosexual marriage and "traditional" family. Andrew summed up the argument this way: "I think, again, [same-sex adoption] is redefining basic community terms. Children are a product of man and woman coming together. . . . I think it's disjointed emotionally, physiologically; it's like wanting the benefit of the union of man and women, but not wanting to unify men and women. Children come about from men and women coming together. . . . I think [same-sex adoption] will confuse sexual identity [for children]." Andrew's argument displayed the multiple reasons evangelical Protestants opposed same-sex adoption.

First, Andrew clearly stated that, like same-sex marriage, same-sex adoption is "redefining" what it means to be a family and a community. Based on their interpretation of the Bible, many evangelical Protestants believed there was only one way for the family to look—a man and a woman with biological children. Additionally, evangelical Protestants suggested that the Bible clearly lays out the roles that a man and a woman are supposed to assume in the family, with the man being the breadwinner and head of the household and the woman taking care of the family and home while also deferring to her husband's authority. Evangelical interviewees feared that if same-sex couples adopted children, the roles within the family would be confused or unfulfilled, thus breaking down the foundation of society—"traditional" family.

Second, and relatedly, because it takes a man and a woman to make a child biologically, evangelical Protestants reasoned that God must have intended only for men and women to raise children together. Consequently, Andrew argued that it is not emotionally healthy for parents to start a family that goes against what God intended. He went as far as to argue that being raised by same-sex parents would confuse children about their own sexuality. Although this belief is not supported by research, many evangelical Protestants were afraid that by allowing same-sex adoption, more children would end up identifying as gay or lesbian.

Finally, Andrew made the argument that same-sex adoption amounted to gay and lesbian people wanting the benefits of heterosexual marriage without doing the work. Another evangelical Protestant, Darlene, concurred; she expounded that by "choosing" a homosexual relationship, gay and lesbian people "give up that natural right" to have children. This argument has been claimed by the Christian Right and implies that gay and lesbian people are seeking "special rights or benefits" rather than equality. To some, raising a child who does not biologically hold the DNA of both parents appears to be a special allowance, but this ignores the fact that many heterosexual couples, by choice or circumstance, adopt, use sperm/egg donors, or employ surrogates.

Another evangelical Protestant, Candace, agreed with Andrew that same-sex adoption would confuse children, but Candace's main concern was that children would not properly learn how to be men or women or how to treat the opposite sex. She explained, "We learn from our parents. . . . You've got a female who's trying to fill the role of a father, then I just don't believe there's any way that that person can adequately do that, especially if they have a son or even a daughter, because the daughter's relationship with her father is so key as far as how she will look for a husband and how she will even treat her husband when she gets married. . . . I think it opens the door for confusion." Regina, an evangelical Protestant, agreed that children would not know if they were "supposed to be masculine or feminine" if they were raised by same-sex couples. She explained that if gay and lesbian people were allowed to adopt, they were "going to do more damage to that child, and it's a selfish move." This line of reasoning is in direct opposition to those who argued that same-sex adoption is acceptable although not ideal. None of the respondents who felt this way indicated it was selfish for same-sex couples to adopt; on the contrary, the respondents in the following category felt that if gay and lesbian couples could provide love for children, then they should be allowed to adopt.

Better Than Nothing: Same-Sex Adoption Is Not What God Intended, but Children Need Love

Though the interviewees in this group felt that same-sex adoption was neither ideal nor what God intended, they supported it because they felt it was better than a child having no parents or being raised in a failing foster care system. These respondents appeared to truly struggle with what is best for children, and their answers demonstrated more ambivalence than those who supported or opposed same-sex adoption.

While only two evangelical Protestants and two mainline Protestants indicated same-sex adoption is acceptable but not ideal, the majority of Catholics (seven of eleven) felt this way. Some individuals in this category went further than simply stating that same-sex adoption was not ideal and indicated that there should be restrictions placed on same-sex couples who adopt. They felt that gay and lesbian people were responsible for taking extra precautions to ensure the safety and well-being of their children. This sentiment paralleled that of Catholics who placed conditions on gay and lesbian people who held leadership positions in the church. Many of the Catholics interviewed were committed to conditional inclusion, supporting requirements for gay and lesbian people before allowing them to qualify for the same rights as their heterosexual peers. However, despite Catholics' belief that same-sex adoption is not ideal, no Catholic interviewees were completely opposed to same-sex adoption or indicated they would vote against it.

There is a lot of baggage wrapped up in this sentiment. First, like those who are fully opposed to same-sex adoption, these respondents demonstrated the importance they placed on traditional gender norms. They suggested there was indeed one proper way to be a man or a woman. Second, it was implied that gay and lesbian people do not know how to be a man or a woman. Once more, gender and sexuality were conflated, and there was the underlying assumption that masculinity is the sole property of heterosexual men and femininity is the sole property of heterosexual women. Finally, the conservative Protestant notion of men and women coming together to make a whole is evident in the arguments of those who supported adoption despite it not being ideal. To become a whole person, these respondents believed, one must have both men and women as direct role models in their life.

Barbara, a mainline Protestant who conditionally supports same-sex adoption, indicated that she supported same-sex adoption because a lot of children need good homes and believed that Christians should "always err on the side of love." Nevertheless, Barbara went on to explain that she was against in vitro fertilization (an assisted reproductive lab procedure where the egg is manually fertilized with the sperm and then transferred into the uterus). She clarified that she is opposed to in vitro fertilization because parents are consciously choosing to deprive their child of the opposite-sex parent: "I believe the best option for a family unit is to have a male and female and children. Because I think each person, each sex, adds to the equation—because males are different, females are different, and each one adds to the family unit in a way that the other one cannot. . . . [Otherwise,] they would miss the characteristics that are inherent in the sex they're missing. . . . I would assume in a same-sex marriage there would be some disruption of those normal patterns of families." So while Barbara would vote in favor of legalizing same-sex adoption, it is clear she does not think same-sex parents are the best families for children and believes that in an "ideal world" this would not be necessary. Clearly, the issue of in vitro fertilization and adoption are two separate issues, but Barbara's opposition to in vitro fertilization clarified her views on same-sex parenting as less than ideal.

According to this argument, the absence of an opposite-sex role model will cause a child to grow up to be confused, incomplete, and/or not a "proper" man or woman. Here the fear of same-sex parents raising gay or lesbian children reappears—if a child does not become a "proper" man or woman, then there is a higher likelihood they will be gay or lesbian in a society where, by definition, being a gay man or a lesbian woman is not the ideal type of masculinity or femininity. (For more about hegemonic masculinity and emphasized femininity, see Connell and Messerschmidt 2005.)

Confusion and ambivalence about the issue of same-sex adoption were clear in Phillip's response as to whether same-sex adoption should be legal. Phillip, a Catholic, said:

> Well, that's a really hard question. . . . I don't think I've come yet to any clear-cut direction on that question because I'm torn like a dichotomy here. You know, I see the sense of compassion for how many of the kids that really need to be adopted there are in this world, and I guess I need to know more about that particular issue. But I just don't know. That's a hard one for me to answer. Although my inclination without making any kind of clear-cut choice, my inclination is to say no. My inclination is to believe that it wouldn't be good for the kid long-term. It might provide a home, it might provide some security, but I don't know that it's going to provide—I really don't know that it's going to provide the kind of psychological and emotional growth that a person needs to really be whole.

Clearly, Phillip was unsure about his beliefs with regards to same-sex adoption. He wanted to do what is in the best interests of children but could not conclude which course of action was correct. After this explanation, Phillip went on to say, "I think there is a wholeness to a man and a woman in a marital relationship, versus two partners of the same sex . . . one just seems more whole than the other, fuller than the other. And why settle for so much less when there is so much more?"

Due to the belief that same-sex adoption is not ideal (or "whole"), some respondents explained that restrictions should be placed on same-sex couples who wish to adopt. Another respondent, Hillary, summed up her conception of conditional acceptance of same-sex adoption and its restrictions this way: "If this was a perfect society where everybody had a mom and dad, then we wouldn't need [same-sex adoption]." But since this is not a perfect society, and children need families, she stated that she would accept gay and lesbian people adopting children. Still, she qualified her acceptance by saying that same-sex parents must ensure there is an opposite-sex mentor in the child's life; otherwise, the child will not know how to properly be a man or a woman.

Whitney, another Catholic, agreed that same-sex adoption would be acceptable "as long as two same-sex parents ensured that child had exposure to a good opposite-sex role model . . . a female influence and a male influence. You become a little more of a holistic person." Catholics in this study felt sympathy for children who needed a home but tempered their full acceptance of same-sex adoption with things they felt gay and lesbian people should do if they intended to adopt—the most important thing being to ensure their children would know how to "properly" be men or women.

All Kids Deserve a Family: Support for Same-Sex Adoption

Some interviewees expressed full acceptance of same-sex adoption and did not feel that it would be detrimental to children in any way. Most mainline Protestants agreed with Isabelle, who said she was fine with same-sex adoption: "There are so many children that need homes, and if they're willing to give a child a home, I don't know why not." In fact, of the nineteen mainline Protestants interviewed, all but three indicated full acceptance of same-sex adoption. Only one mainline Protestant was opposed to same-sex adoption, while two indicated it was not an ideal situation. In addition to the majority of mainline Protestants, four of eleven Catholics also supported the right of same-sex couples to adopt children. Despite mainline Protestants' and Catholics' acceptance of same-sex adoption, their justifications remained complex and at times convoluted. Whereas some felt that same-sex adoption was in the best interests of children and society, others continued to worry about the larger societal consequences of same-sex adoption.

One mainline Protestant, Kelsey, demonstrated the first viewpoint: same-sex adoption is good for children and society. When asked what influence she believed being adopted by a same-sex couple would have on children, she explained, "[Children] will probably be a lot more affirming of who they are and they'll feel a lot freer to be themselves, you know. But I don't think that it's going to, like, create more gay kids or whatever." Kelsey thought being raised in a nontraditional family would give children the opportunity to be more open-minded and accepting. She clearly rejected the idea that a child's sexuality would be influenced by their parents' sexuality.

Tracy and Brad, both mainline Protestants, exemplified the incongruence found between supporting same-sex marriage versus same-sex adoption. While neither Tracy nor Brad supported same-sex marriage, they both felt that same-sex adoption should be legal and would not be harmful to children. Tracy explained that same-sex couples should have the right to adopt because "studies have shown that children in a homosexual, stable, loving household are just as well off as kids in heterosexual, stable, loving households, and better than kids in other situations." Similarly, Brad believed that "anybody that passes the background checks and that's loving and can provide a stable home, you know, should be able to adopt." This incongruence shows the difference between supporting marriage, especially as a religious institution, and supporting adoption. While some mainline Protestants and Catholics felt that marriage should be reserved for a partnership between a man and a woman, because that is what God intended, they also supported the right of same-sex couples to raise children. They felt that the Christian response to this specific right had to be what was in the best interests of children and that having a loving family was more important than the gender or sexuality of the parents.

Essentially, the primary issue mainline Protestants raised about same-sex adoption was that other children and/or their parents may pick on a child with same-sex parents. This was one point on which they tended to agree with both evangelical Protestants and Catholics. All three groups said, "Children can be cruel," but for mainline Protestants, this was not enough of a justification to disallow same-sex couples from adopting.

* * * * *

In all, more Mississippi Christians supported same-sex adoption than same-sex marriage. This could be in part because some respondents understood the dire need to help children in the state of Mississippi. In 2017, Mississippi again ranked last in the nation for overall child well-being (Annie E. Casey Foundation 2017). This ranking is partially based on the fact that Mississippi has the highest child poverty rate in the country: approximately 31 percent of Mississippi children were living in poverty in 2015 (Annie E. Casey Foundation 2017). Due to poverty and other issues in the state, the foster care system has struggled to keep up with the demand and has been largely failing children. Conditions are so poor in the foster care system in Mississippi that the state is at risk of being the first in the country to have its child welfare system place under outside control (Palmer and Robertson 2016). Compassion and empathy for children led many respondents in this study to support same-sex adoption even if they did not feel it was ideal.

Additionally, same-sex adoption does not require the approval or sanction of a Christian church in the same way that marriage does. Since marriage is viewed as religious by most Christians and as a holy sacrament by Catholics, it is harder to separate the religious implications of marriage from the secular, civil meaning of marriage for many. For this reason, it may be easier to support the civil right of adoption for children who need homes. Nevertheless, the religious implications of family and gender are still clear for those who oppose same-sex adoption or only support it conditionally. Most respondents in this study still believed in gender essentialism and the "traditional" family. They felt that the ideal way to raise children was in a heterosexual, nuclear family.

Since the main subcultural identity boundary around conservative Christianity today is sexuality rather than gender, some respondents were willing to allow same-sex adoption as long as the parents could raise heterosexual children. Because about half of children in Mississippi are being raised by single parents, respondents seemed willing to concede to families that were not "traditional" if parents ensured that their children would grow up with both men and women as role models outside of the home. While for many of the interviewees these circumstances were not ideal, they were better than leaving kids behind with no one to love them.

5

All [Wo]men Are
Created Equal, or Are They?

The Gay and Lesbian Civil Rights Movement

Oh, gosh. There are a whole lot of people I wish would just stay home.
I really think that we can politicize so much stuff that pretty soon
you're just over the whole thing. I think if people would just let things
take their natural course it would work out, so I'm not happy about
a lot of those movements. I just think it's overblown a lot of times.
—Paula, a sixty-six-year-old white mainline Protestant
from the Gulf Coast of Mississippi

Beliefs and attitudes regarding same-sex marriage and same-sex adoption generally fall along the lines of religious ideology. On the contrary, beliefs about the overall gay and lesbian civil rights movement seem less predictable.[1] While the respondents in this study had more comprehensive views and opinions about *specific* rights being sought by gay and lesbian people, they held more negative and ambiguous attitudes toward the gay and lesbian social movement for equality.

While the history of the gay and lesbian civil rights movement in the United States dates back to the 1950s and the "homophile movement" (Carter 2010), the beginning of the modern-day gay and lesbian civil rights movement is usually identified with the

Stonewall Inn Riots of June 1969. The Stonewall Inn, a popular gay bar in Greenwich Village, New York, was raided by police on June 27, 1969. Instead of going quietly, the patrons—mostly young gay men of color, many of whom identified as transgender or drag queens—stood up and fought back against police harassment with three nights of rioting.[2] These riots sparked a worldwide movement for gay and lesbian civil rights. In fact, Carter (2010) argues that the significant victories for gay and lesbian rights around the world can be traced to 1969, when "gay people found the courage to stand up for themselves on the streets of Greenwich Village" (266). Other similar victories in the United States include removing homosexuality from the American Psychiatric Association's Diagnostic and Statistical Manual of mental disorders in 1973, the decriminalization of "homosexual conduct" in 2003, and the legalization of same-sex marriage across the nation in 2015.[3] (For a more comprehensive list of gay and lesbian civil rights milestones, see CNN's [2018] "LGBT Rights Milestones Fast Facts.")

Discussions of the gay and lesbian civil rights movement evoked strong feelings and opinions for the respondents in this study regardless of their religious affiliations. While a general trend still emerges from the interviews—with evangelical Protestants holding the most negative opinions, Catholics being more indecisive, and mainline Protestants showing the most support for gay and lesbian rights—the lines are not as clear-cut as they are on specific rights. The interviewees generally agreed that the gay and lesbian civil rights movement is divisive and could be more productive if it were carried out in a different way. For example, Phillip, a Catholic interviewee, told me that he feels the movement is "creating polarization more and more, and that's never going to be the answer."

The Gay and Lesbian Civil Rights Movement: A Sign of Disaster

Of those interviewed, nine evangelical Protestants, four Catholics, and one mainline Protestant suggested that the movement for gay and lesbian equality will have only negative influences on society. These respondents felt that the gay and lesbian civil rights movement is sign of forthcoming disaster. Six of ten evangelical Protestant respondents used the terms "dangerous," "detrimental," or "extreme" when discussing the gay and lesbian civil rights movement. On the contrary, no mainline Protestants used these terms, and only two Catholics discussed the movement using the similar terms "militant" and "scary."

Erica, an evangelical Protestant, explained that she understands why gay and lesbian people are fighting, but even though she could not think of a specific example, she was sure "the more you go down that road [toward gay and lesbian equality], it's going to lead to more and more destruction." Darlene, an evangelical Protestant, believed that due to the movement for equality, "more extreme groups would want to get rights, like, you know, polygamists or pedophiles." Candace, another evangelical Protestant, explained that we are entering a "dangerous season." She said, "I feel like we're really entering a real dangerous season because it seems like the direction [gay and lesbian people] want to go is making it illegal for me to express my belief on that lifestyle and how I believe it's unhealthy. . . . I've sure watched a lot of pressure being applied to companies like Chick-Fil-A and I can only believe that if this keeps going on like this, you know we [Christians] won't be able to stand on what we believe is true." In her interview, Candace displayed pronounced fear due to the gay and lesbian civil rights movement. She believed she would no longer be allowed to express her religious beliefs and that, if things kept progressing toward equality for gay and lesbian people, she would eventually end up in prison for believing that gay and lesbian people are living a "lifestyle" of sin. The Christian Right often uses these fear tactics to gain the support of conservative Christians. This intense fear ensures that Candace will continue to fight against gay and lesbian equality.

The sentiments held by these evangelical Protestants are not surprising, considering that evangelicals have been at the forefront of the antigay movement since the late 1970s (Fetner 2001, 2008). The Christian antigay movement seeks to prevent gay and lesbian citizens from gaining additional civil rights and to overturn those won since the beginning of the gay and lesbian rights movement. Many of the respondents in this study came of age during the beginnings of this antigay Christian backlash.

This is why Candace was proud of her support of the Christian Right and felt it was through Christian organizations that she could get valid information on family and society. When I asked Candace if she has ever supported political Christian groups, she was happy to say that she had. She told me about why she supports political Christian organizations:

> I have supported American Family Radio because I love the fact that I can actually find out some information that's *not biased* by the society that's trying to pull everybody away from God. And I've also sent money to Focus on the Family, because I do believe families are very important, and for a while there, they really didn't get that much involved in politics. But when it started to affect family and we could see the judgments were being made that were going to hurt the family, I was really proud of Dr. Dobson for speaking out. . . . I support it because they try to make a difference in families. I've given some money to Heritage Foundation, because I do believe that they are trying to get the truth out about the importance of walking a godly life and making godly choices. (Emphasis added)

In addition to her pastor, Candace received much of her information from right-wing Christian organizations. These organizations are in clear opposition to gay and lesbian equality and spread fear about the threat of gay and lesbian people to society. Candace had clearly bought into the message that gay and lesbian rights are a zero-sum game and that if gay and lesbian people gain equality, all Christians will lose—and lose big. Hence Candace believed that Christians must not be swayed by secular society to support gay and lesbian people; they must stand strong in their opposition—for their own protection and the protection of the world at large.

Candace was not alone in these beliefs. David, an evangelical Protestant, also explained how the gay and lesbian civil rights movement is dangerous. He believed the gay and lesbian civil rights movement is "detrimental to the U[nited] S[tates]. I think it's detrimental to any society. They're wishing to demand *special privileges* for a class of people and economically speaking the lesbian, gay section of the country makes much higher salaries on average than the *normal* heterosexuals do.[4] So to say that they are a class that's being discriminated against economically is a bunch of baloney" (emphasis added). David believed that gay and lesbian people are fighting not for equality but rather to have more rights than heterosexual people. Although this claim has no basis in fact, David was convinced that gay and lesbian people are trying to move ahead of heterosexuals and must be stopped. Another interviewee, Regina, agreed, venting, "I'm tired of getting it stuffed down my throat. . . . So, you're homosexual. Does that give you a special class? You're saying, like, 'I'm special.' You're just like anybody else. It amazes me. I really can't get over that."

While some evangelical Protestant disapproval and fear was based in self-interest and the belief that gay and lesbian people are trying to get ahead of them, there was also the fear that the gay and lesbian civil rights movement would bring about the end of the world. Angela, an evangelical Protestant, explained, "I feel that things that happen to this nation, like earthquakes and hurricanes and all of that kind of stuff—I feel like that God allows those things to happen because he's trying to get our attention, and so I feel like that some of those things would be happening, just like how Katrina hit New Orleans and almost wiped it out. You know, God was trying to get the people in New Orleans' attention and the people down on the coast. So, I think some of those things would continue happening." I asked if Angela was referring to indications of the End Times, and she confirmed that was what she meant. She genuinely felt that granting gay and lesbian people the right to marry, adopt, or march in the streets would provoke the wrath of God. Angela believed that natural disasters were a direct result of the debauchery that the gay and lesbian civil rights movement showcased.

POSITIVE BENEFITS OF THE GAY AND LESBIAN CIVIL RIGHTS MOVEMENT

Fourteen of the forty respondents interviewed believed the gay and lesbian civil rights movement would have only negative impacts on society; exactly the same number of respondents believed the movement would have only positive impacts on society. Namely, eleven mainline Protestants and three Catholics discussed the positive benefits the movement has had or can have on society. Kelsey, a mainline Protestant, explained, "I think [the gay and lesbian civil rights movement] is really exciting, and I personally feel like there's the work of the Holy Spirit, that God is involved in this." Another mainline Protestant, Marie, described the movement this way: "Just like any other civil rights [movement], [gay and lesbian people] are just demanding their rights. . . . Some people will open their eyes to the reality [that being gay or lesbian] is OK, and some will just go deeper into their hatred." Similarly, Kelsey believed the gay and lesbian civil rights movement is necessary, especially for education purposes. Kelsey clarified, "I think education always brings about change and any time that. . . . a person can stand up, talk, share a story—that may help to change another person's perspective and thoughts. So, I believe offering platforms for that to happen for people who are gay, lesbian, bisexual, transgender, whatever—to have a place where they can interact with people who don't necessarily feel the same as them and try to share their story is an exceedingly positive thing."

Like Marie and Kelsey, other respondents felt the gay and lesbian civil rights movement has had positive effects on society and emphasized the need for the LGBTQ community to be visible and stand up for their rights. Some of the respondents in this category compared the gay and lesbian civil rights movement to the African American civil rights movement and explained that it was time for LGBTQ people to receive equality. None of the interviewees in this category saw the movement as a sign of disaster or discussed potential negative outcomes of the movement. These respondents did not feel that gay and lesbian people were trying to offend them; rather, they saw the movement as educational or even as a sign of God's power working through gay and lesbian people.

MIXED REVIEWS OF THE GAY AND LESBIAN
CIVIL RIGHTS MOVEMENT

Six interviewees—two Catholics and four mainline Protestants—felt that the gay and lesbian civil rights movement would have mixed results for society. These interviewees appreciated the need for the gay and lesbian civil rights movement but felt that it crossed the line when it impinged on their religious beliefs. Many of these respondents supported the fight for equal rights under the law, but when gay and lesbian people sought equal recognition within their church or denomination, some drew the line. Ervin, a mainline Protestant, held this view: "If you're pursuing something civilly, I have no beef against that . . . but if you're talking about other aspects of the movement in terms of, you know, an acceptance, or if you're talking about the fight against the church's perspective, then I would be on the other side of that line." Ervin believed that gay and lesbian people should be allowed to fight for their rights but that they do not have the right to ask others to change their religious beliefs about the issue.

Other respondents who could see potential positives and negatives of the movement had concerns about what this movement would mean for children. Ervin and others explained that the movement for gay and lesbian equality would cause children to be more open to homosexuality as an "easy alternative." Lauren, a forty-three-year-old white evangelical Protestant from the Mississippi Delta, expanded on this sentiment: "From what I've noticed around here, a lot of younger people are choosing to become homosexual, and sometimes it scares me because they're so young. I feel like they're influenced by their schools. . . . Sometimes I wonder if it's more like teen smoking; it's cool to do it." Similarly, Brenda, a Catholic, said she supported part of the gay and lesbian movement but with limitations: "I don't know if we need to bring it down to the high school levels, as far as this gay alliance movement. . . . We don't have heterosexual movements in schools; the gay and bi alliances aren't necessary at a high school level." Again, the conditional acceptance of some Catholics becomes obvious. Brenda was supportive of gay and lesbian adults receiving equal rights, but she stopped short of teaching children and teens about issues relating to sexuality. The idea of "special rights" also slipped back into the conversation. Brenda believed gay and lesbian people were seeking special rights by having gay alliance movements in high schools while there were no "heterosexual movements" in schools. This is not the first time this argument has been made; it is comparable to the current push for "men's studies" in colleges.

THE GAY AND LESBIAN WHAT?

The remaining six interviewees indicated they did not know enough about the gay and lesbian civil rights movement to predict its implications. For instance, one Catholic respondent, Tim, said, "Honestly I don't know anything about it. I'm too involved in my own life." Gretchen, a mainline Protestant, explained, "You know, I don't know anybody involved with [the gay and lesbian civil rights movement]. . . . The [gay and lesbian people] that I know are very comfortable with their lives. They're very successful people and they aren't out fighting a lot of wars about it. They've moved past it. And so . . . if they're involved with it, they have not mentioned it to me." These respondents either did not care enough to pay attention to the movement or felt it was for LGBTQ people who weren't as comfortable with themselves as the respondents' gay and lesbian friends and family members.

If You've Got It, Flaunt It: Pride Parades

Overall, much of the resistance to the gay and lesbian civil rights movement seemed to stem from the conflation of the entire struggle for gay and lesbian civil rights with gay pride parades. The first gay pride parade was held in New York City in June of 1970 to honor the one-year anniversary of the Stonewall Riots (PBS 2011). Since then, annual gay pride parades have become a universal staple. In fact, in 2017 there were over four hundred gay pride parades scheduled around the world (Gay Pride Calendar 2017). Pride parades began as "radical marches" for equality, but they have evolved over the last three decades into more "festive parades" (PBS 2011). These events usually are the culmination of a weeklong celebration of gay pride. Most parades include festive floats, a march, entertainment (usually including drag shows), and speakers (often politicians and prominent figures in the civil rights movement). These parades commemorate LGBTQ history and celebrate the diversity within the community (PBS 2011).

The evolution of gay pride parades from political marches to celebratory parades has garnered severe criticism from those who oppose gay and lesbian equality. The Christian Right, and conservatives more generally, often point to these parades as evidence of the depravity of the gay and lesbian community. Certain events that take place at gay pride parades, such as drag shows and public displays of affection between same-sex couples, are used to condemn the broader gay and lesbian civil rights movement. Even among some of the respondents who supported gay and lesbian equality, conflating gay pride parades with the entire gay and lesbian civil rights movement led to negative beliefs and attitudes toward the movement.

For instance, one mainline Protestant, Jason, who was fully supportive of same-sex marriage and adoption, had negative feelings about the civil rights movement more generally. He explained, "I have some resistance. . . . I don't want to use the word flaunting, but I don't flaunt my sexuality. . . . Public displays, phallics, and that sort of stuff—I'm opposed to that kind of glorification. I would want you to have equal rights. I would want you to be able to be married and have a partner . . . [but] I think it's superfluous, and I think it denigrates . . . and sexualizes it more than it's necessary." As this comment suggests, when Jason heard the phrase "gay and lesbian civil rights movement," it brought to mind what are, to him, eccentric or even offensive parades. The idea of "flaunting" one's sexuality persisted throughout the discussions of gay and lesbian civil rights, and many people could not move past the idea of sexual promiscuity and the "glorification" of same-sex sexual activity. This celebration of sexuality was too much even for many supportive mainline Protestants.

In addition to "flaunting," some respondents explained they felt the gay and lesbian civil rights movement was too outlandish. They described feeling like gay and lesbian rights were being "stuffed down their throat[s]" or of being "slapped upside the head" with gay and lesbian sexuality. One Catholic, Susan, summed it up like this: "Some demonstrations and stuff for gay civil rights and stuff are just so outlandishly out there. It's just like, you feel slapped upside the head with it." Hillary, another Catholic, agreed. When I asked for her views about the gay and lesbian civil rights move-ment, she discussed a conversation she had with her brother, who is gay: "'Why do you guys have to be so flamboyant? Why do you have to go out there and have this parade, and dress weird, and color your hair weird? If anything, it just makes you look like you're weird.' . . . I just wish they would keep quiet about it and go about their own business. I don't go out there and advertise my sexual relationships." The Mississippi Christians I interviewed had a hard time understanding why gay pride parades are necessary for the LGBTQ community. They compared these events to their own sexuality and could not comprehend why gay and lesbian people feel the need to celebrate their sexuality. Hillary was concerned that her brother was only making things worse for himself by tak-ing part in these events. She appeared to genuinely want what was best for her brother, but she could not wrap her head around this need for celebration. Like many Catholics in this study, Hillary wished that gay and lesbian people could just keep their sexuality to themselves and go about their lives. This reaction to the gay and lesbian civil rights movement ignored the fact that gay and lesbian people (and others in the LGBTQ community) have been forced to stay quiet and closeted throughout history. It missed the point that this celebration of gay and lesbian history and community once a year may be the only time that gay and lesbian people feel accepted, especially in the South.

Comparison to the African American Civil Rights Movement

Another point of contention among interviewees was whether the gay and lesbian civil rights movement is similar to the African American civil rights movement of the 1960s. There was no direct question in the interview about how the gay and lesbian civil rights movement compares to civil rights movements of the past, but nine out of the forty respondents spontaneously mentioned the African American civil rights movement. Five interviewees discussed the similarities between the two movements, and four discussed how the movements were different.

Four mainline Protestants and one Catholic brought up similarities between the African American civil rights movement and the gay and lesbian civil rights movement. Isabelle, a mainline Protestant who identified as African American, told me that she believed gay and lesbian people are "piggybacking on the civil rights from the sixties with, you know, the black issue and having the freedom to be able to have equal access to everything. I think if they don't speak out, they won't be heard. . . . I would hope that we could all live here as human beings and respect each other." Kelsey, a white mainline Protestant, agreed with Isabelle that the movement is similar to the racial civil rights movement of the 1960s and said it gave her a "really joyful, hopeful feeling." Finally, Leo, another white mainline Protestant, explained, "I wish it weren't necessary, but it's time. . . . If Martin Luther King was with us he'd be saying, 'Okay, it's time to hit the repeat button.'" These mainline Mississippi Protestants showed respect for the gay and lesbian civil rights movement and believed it was a necessity, like the African American civil rights movement. They saw the movement as a sign of hope and progress. This was not the case for most of the respondents in this study. Even calling this movement a civil rights struggle aroused powerful feelings of opposition among some respondents. Many of these interviewees felt the gay and lesbian civil rights movement was not as difficult or as serious as the African American civil rights movement.

One Catholic, one mainline Protestant, and two evangelical Protestant respondents, all of whom identified as white, explained that comparing the gay and lesbian civil rights movement to the African American civil rights movement was problematic at best. Rick, a Catholic, said he felt gay and lesbian people are not "going to have as much struggle, or at least I hope they're not going to have as much struggle, as African Americans did. . . . I mean it's more of a 'Hi, we're here' kind of thing, which I think is a good thing. I mean, I think we've progressed a lot." Rick was not arguing that the gay and lesbian civil rights movement is not necessary or is bad for society, but he believed it is not comparable to the African American civil rights movement. He argued that gay and lesbian people just need to be acknowledged and known to end prejudice and discrimination. Rick did not believe this would be the same kind of fight African Americans endured; rather, as he said, gay and lesbian people just needed to say, "Hi, we're here." Rick thought society had progressed to a point where minority groups would be accepted once they made their struggles known.

In a more negative manner, one evangelical Protestant, Caleb, explained that he was not concerned with the gay and lesbian civil rights movement. His answer conveyed a level of frustration with the gay and lesbian movement and especially with its being compared to the African American civil rights movement:

I think [the gay and lesbian civil rights movement] is slightly ridiculous, because I don't want to say [gay and lesbian people] have an agenda, but it feels like that sometimes. Because I am a straight, heterosexual, conservative Christian, I feel like I'm looked at as ignorant because of it sometimes. Also, the fact that they compare themselves to the civil rights movement of the 1960s, I'm kind of offended by that because in that case there was open hangings of black people. There were riots in the street where police were setting dogs on people and spraying them down with water hoses. I don't see that happening to gay people in America. So, I don't like the extremism that they take in comparing themselves to the civil rights movement of the sixties, but if they feel strongly about it, then by all means. I'm not concerned with the culture of America per se.

Unpacking Caleb's statement about the gay and lesbian civil rights movement indicates he was at least somewhat concerned about the movement's implications. Caleb used the catchphrase "agenda"—often invoked by the Christian Right—in his response to indicate malicious intent in the movement. "Agenda" suggests that gay and lesbian people have some ulterior motive rather than merely seeking equality and basic human rights. It is another term that begets fear among conservative Christians with the implication that gay and lesbian people are out to harm Christians and society at large. Caleb went on to say that as a (white) heterosexual, conservative Christian, he felt that he was looked down on or, in his words, "looked at as ignorant." Caleb's identity epitomizes privilege in the United States, especially in the South, but the gay and lesbian civil rights movement caused him to feel discriminated against. This is the same sentiment Candace expressed earlier, when she explained that she was fearful of being thrown in jail for her Christian beliefs if the gay and lesbian civil rights movement were to succeed.

Finally, Caleb clarified why comparing the gay and lesbian civil rights movement to the African American civil rights movement is misleading. He said he is even "offended" by this comparison even though he is white. The justification behind this offense was that gay and lesbian people are not being physically harassed to the same degree that African Americans were in the 1960s. Therefore, in his estimation, the gay and lesbian civil rights movement is based in "extremism" and exaggeration. Caleb believed that if people are not being hanged or beaten in the streets, then a civil rights movement is unnecessary. Interestingly, after all this, Caleb still maintained that he was not concerned about American culture.

Mainline Protestants in this study indicated more support of the gay and lesbian civil rights movements than Catholics and evangelical Protestants, and their answers aligned more closely with the changing views within secular society. As Smith et al. (1998) describe, these answers show engagement with society but not distinction from it. Mainline Protestants did not place conditions on gay and lesbian rights and were more likely to argue that the gay and lesbian civil rights movement has positive benefits for society. Their own Protestant religion was not used to distinguish them from gay and lesbian people or to justify different rights for themselves than for gay and lesbian people.

Catholics' answers also showed their engagement with society. Overall, their responses departed more from secular views than the responses of mainline Protestants. Catholics were torn about how to approach gay and lesbian rights. Most Catholics indicated a desire to grant gay and lesbian people equality, yet they nevertheless wished to hold onto the conservative teachings of the Catholic Church that indicate the act of homosexuality is sinful. Catholics' competing ideologies—desire for both equality and the conservative teachings of the Catholic Church—often led respondents to a place of conditional acceptance. As in the church, where conditions are placed on gay and lesbian people in leadership positions, Catholics took a middle road on gay and lesbian rights. Often they supported civil unions but not marriage in the church. They supported same-sex adoption but placed conditions on how gay and lesbian parents should raise their children. Finally, they were divided on whether the gay and lesbian civil rights movement has a positive or negative influence on society.

Lastly, when it came to the issue of gay and lesbian rights, evangelical Protestants again presented a high level of engagement with, but distinction from, secular society (Smith et al. 1998). In this sample, respondents indicated almost complete opposition to same-sex marriage, same-sex adoption, and the gay and lesbian civil rights movement. They struggled to set themselves apart from gay and lesbian people and those who support gay and lesbian rights. The issues surrounding gay and lesbian rights were used as a boundary to protect their embattled Christian identity. Whether their concern was minor or regarded the end of the world, evangelical Protestants described great fear and concern about what gay and lesbian rights meant for society. This lines up with previous research that shows evangelical Protestants are more likely to condemn homosexuality, more likely to hold prejudicial attitudes toward gay and lesbian people, and less likely to support gay and lesbian civil rights (Bramlett 2012; Duck and Hunsberger 1999; Hill et al. 2010; Sherkat et al. 2011).

One task for activists and those seeking equality for gay and lesbian people more generally is to determine what may change or soften these views against gay and lesbian equality and make conservative Christians more open to gay and lesbian civil rights. Previous research indicates that knowing someone who is gay or lesbian should have a positive influence on overcoming negative perceptions and attitudes toward gay and lesbian rights. In the next section, I examine how having a friend or family member who identifies as gay or lesbian influenced Mississippi Christians' views about gay and lesbian rights.

PART 3

Social Contact with Gay and Lesbian People

6

Some of My Best Friends Are Gay

The Influence of Social Contact

[Having gay and lesbian friends and family members] gave me a more informed view and a closer, more personal view than what I had before, which was basically just a stereotype.... I think that definitely that kind of change in beliefs and more open behavior can come about when we have personal relationships with other people.
—Victor, a forty-three-year-old white mainline Protestant from northeast Mississippi

Knowing someone who is gay or lesbian, especially if they are a friend or relative, has been shown to reduce heterosexuals' negative beliefs and attitudes about homosexuality. Activists continue to argue that coming out to friends and family will have positive political impacts for gay and lesbian civil rights (Lewis 2011). My own coming out story anecdotally supports this research. Although the positive results of coming out were not immediate for me, eventually my family accepted my sexuality and slowly began to change their attitudes and beliefs about homosexuality and gay and lesbian equality. While I grew up in a mainline Protestant congregation—which are generally more accepting of LGBTQ individuals—being in the rural South meant there was still a strong vein of conservatism within my congregation. However, the more lenient interpretation of the Bible and the heavy emphasis on the importance of love eventually won out in my story. Though some members of my family may never fully see my relationship with my wife as morally correct or equal to their marriages, after some time, they have all accepted and continued to love me. The threat of ostracism that I feared as a child and the belief that homosexuality was sinful were overcome when my family realized I was a lesbian and they'd had time to deal with the discrepancy between what they expected and what occurred. I was extremely lucky, but I cannot say this was the case for many of my friends who grew up in more conservative religious environments.

Social Contact with Gay and Lesbian People

Social contact theory suggests that when people get to know those in different groups, this has the potential to encourage more accurate and positive beliefs and attitudes about others (Allport 1954). By learning accurate information about another group, people are able to correct negative stereotypes they hold and, in turn, reduce prejudice (Pettigrew 1998).[1] Thus when conservative Christians learn more accurate information about gay and lesbian people, this should help to reduce negative stereotypes and prejudices toward this group. Additionally, Pettigrew (1998) argues that when people interact with those who are different from themselves, they usually change their behavior to at least appear nice and friendly. According to Pettigrew, these changes in behavior, even if they are forced, can lead to changes in attitudes. If conservative Christians behave in a polite and respectful manner toward gay and lesbian individuals, eventually these actions may modify their overall behavior and reduce prejudice. So maybe some of the Southern charm and "Bless your hearts" could lead to real changes in the attitudes of conservative Christians. Finally, Pettigrew claimed that continued contact with gay and lesbian people has the potential to reduce anxiety and increase positive emotions toward this group. For instance, an individual's empathy toward a friend or relative who is gay or lesbian could help to improve attitudes toward this population more generally (Pettigrew 1998; Pettigrew et al. 2011).

Overall, social contact theory suggests that increased interaction between Mississippi Christians and gay and lesbian people should lead to less prejudicial beliefs and attitudes as well as increased support for gay and lesbian civil rights—same-sex marriage, same-sex adoption, and so on.

MY FRIEND IS GAY, BUT . . .

Two decades of research on the influences of social contact with gay and lesbian people have produced varied results. Lewis (2011) found that even with groups who have a lower probability of supporting gay and lesbian rights, such as conservative Christians, social contact still had a positive influence. He went on to explain that the relationship between social contact and support of gay and lesbian rights even holds for political conservatives and evangelical Protestants, although the influences were weaker for these groups. On the contrary, Bramlett (2012) found that social contact did not have a positive influence on the opinions of white Protestants (mainline or evangelical) with regards to same-sex marriage. Bramlett (2012) discovered, however, that having a gay friend or family member does increase the likelihood of supporting same-sex marriage among individuals in different cultures and religious traditions, such as Latino Catholics, black Protestants, and to a lesser degree, white Catholics. Similarly, in a previous study conducted by Brauner-Otto and myself (2015), we found that the positive influences of social contact were seen to a lesser degree among evangelical Protestants with gay or lesbian friends than in the larger society. Our study indicated that evangelical Protestants were only half as likely as nonevangelicals to believe that homosexuality is morally acceptable, and it also indicated that social contact had no influence on evangelical Protestants' beliefs about the origins of homosexuality (Baker and Brauner-Otto 2015); that is, whether or not they have a friend who identifies as gay or lesbian, evangelical Protestants were still far more likely to believe that homosexuality is a choice rather than the influence of environmental factors or an inborn trait. This is important because Christians' view of the origins of homosexuality is directly related to their support or opposition to gay and lesbian civil rights. The more a person believes homosexuality is a choice, the more likely they are to oppose gay and lesbian rights.

In this study, I expand on social contact theory by focusing on what Pettigrew and Tropp (2006) refer to as "negative features" that prevent or discourage social contact between groups from decreasing prejudicial attitudes. As Pettigrew and Tropp (2006) explain, previous research focused on the features of social contact that reduce prejudice has largely ignored factors that cause social contact to be ineffective. Hodson, Harry, and Mitchell (2009) argue that the current research on social contact theory has generally ignored the impact of social contact on "prejudice-prone individuals." If there are negative features that render social contact less effective, previous literature may "have underestimated contact effects, particularly among people most in need of prejudice interventions, those higher in prejudice" (Hodson, Harry, and Mitchell 2009, 509). For this reason, I attempt to determine what factor(s) render these relationships ineffective—or at least less effective—among evangelical Protestants and conservative Catholics.

"COUNTERVAILING ETHICAL IMPERATIVES": JUDGMENT OR COMPASSION

One possible negative feature that deters the reduction of prejudice toward gay and lesbian people among conservative Christians is their subcultural identity. Because conservative Christians use antihomosexuality as a subcultural identity boundary to separate themselves from society, having gay or lesbian friends or family members may not lead to the same positive results as it does for other people. Opposition to homosexuality is an integral part of conservative Christians' religious identity, and so having a friend or family member who is gay or lesbian may not be enough to change their beliefs and attitudes about homosexuality—or at least not to the same degree. When conservative Christians try to balance the importance of their personal relationships with gay and lesbian people against their religious identity, adherence to strict biblical literalism and/or church authority often outweighs the positive influences of social contact with gay and lesbian people.

Additional factors that may deter the positive benefits of social contact are Christians' "countervailing ethical imperatives" of judgment and compassion (Bartkowski and Regis 2003, 17). In an ethnographic study of faith-based poverty relief, Bartkowski and Regis (2003) argued that when congregations try to combine these two contradictory obligations, it can lead to varied understandings of justice. The moral imperative of judgment within Christianity is based on social distinctions constructed through boundaries—that is, subcultural identity. In contrast, compassion is based on principles of equality and mutuality (Bartkowski and Regis 2003). When considering beliefs and attitudes toward homosexuality and gay and lesbian rights, the same balancing of judgment and compassion is present.

While mainline Protestants and liberal Catholics generally place emphasis on compassion, equality, and mutuality, evangelical Protestants and conservative Catholics stress the importance of distinction through judgment. Therefore compassion for gay and lesbian friends and family members may lead mainline Protestants and liberal Catholics to accept gay and lesbian rights, while the need for distinctive identities and boundaries may lead evangelical Protestants and conservative Catholics to draw the line at gay and lesbian rights. Both groups use Christian ethics in their decisions on how to handle issues of homosexuality and gay and lesbian rights; the difference, however, is that each is focused on a different obligation. As Bartkowski and Regis (2003) explain, the combination of these seemingly contradictory obligations leads to extremely different understandings of justice. Having a friend or relative who identifies as gay or lesbian plays an important role for Christians who weigh the moral imperative of compassion over judgment, but for those Christians who thrive on an embattled identity through distinction (Smith et al. 1998), labeling and condemnation often outweigh compassion in the battle for morality.

Applying Social Contact Research to
Mississippi Christians' Beliefs and Attitudes

Does subcultural identity, especially among conservative Christians, outweigh the positive influences of having a gay or lesbian friend or family member? Does a conservative religious identity prevent these relationships from overcoming prejudice? Or can these relationships be enough to overcome the conservative religious beliefs that condemn homosexuality and gay and lesbian civil rights?

Social contact can be measured in a number of ways; for this study, I define social contact as having a gay or lesbian friend or family member.[2] While the closeness of relationships and the number of relationships matter, any amount of positive social contact should decrease prejudice and lead to more favorable beliefs and attitudes regarding homosexuality and gay and lesbian rights. As a qualitative study, the focus is on how respondents make sense of their relationships with gay and lesbian people rather than the number of those relationships. The discussions I had with interviewees provide vivid illustrations of the struggle between competing and often contradictory identities as a Christian and as a friend or family member of a gay or lesbian person.

Of the forty interviewees, eighteen reported having a gay or lesbian family member, and thirty-one reported having a gay or lesbian friend. Family relationships ranged from a respondent's own child to their stepchild's relative. Interview participants were chosen because they indicated having a friend or relative who identified as gay or lesbian on a prior survey, but interestingly, when asked about relationships with gay and lesbian people, six interviewees stated they did not have any relationships with gay or lesbian people. This suggests that surveys may overestimate actual social contact with gay and lesbian people. When asked to discuss their relationships with gay or lesbian people, four out of six respondents who reported no relationships either forgot to mention family members they had claimed on the survey or described the people they knew as acquaintances or coworkers, not friends.

Two of these six interviewees were evangelical Protestants who explained this discrepancy by describing their relationships with "formerly" gay or lesbian people—friends who had "struggled" with homosexuality but now identify as heterosexual.

Though most interviewees had gay or lesbian friends or relatives, the majority described the relationships as distant and rarely communicated with these friends or relatives. One potential reason for lack of communication was the friends' or family members' fear of coming out. Many respondents stated that their friend or relative was afraid to tell them about their sexuality or that the respondent themselves avoided contact for fear of saying the wrong thing. For example, Brenda, a Catholic, explained that her brother-in-law is gay but has never felt comfortable coming out to the family: "He was never comfortable enough to reveal his sexual orientation to our family, to my husband's family. So, I think it's always been kind of implied, I don't think I ever was told, 'Oh, you know he's gay.' But, just getting to know him, and know the family, and know that he's had a roommate the last fifteen years, and knowing his roommate and knowing his interactions, it's pretty obvious that he is [gay], although he has never come out to me." This feeling of sexuality being hidden but implicit could cause distance between friends and family members. Brenda described her brother-in-law as having a "roommate" for fifteen years; if no one acknowledged his partner as legitimate, or if he is not invited to family gatherings, it makes sense that close social contact would be difficult to establish.

Another Catholic, Hillary, said her brother delayed telling her that he was gay because he was afraid of what she would think. She explained, "I have twelve brothers and sisters, and I was the last one that he called. I guess he was most fearful of telling me. I don't know why, because that's my little brother, the one that I always looked out after. I guess he didn't want to disappoint me, you know?" The social distance between Mississippi Christians and gay and lesbian people can be a two-way street, with Christians pushing gay or lesbian people away, while at the same time, gay or lesbian people may be purposely creating distance out of fear and to protect themselves from ostracism. Of course, this fear is often justified—when a family member did come out, many respondents did not accept that they were actually gay or lesbian, or they shunned them for it. For example, Erica, an evangelical Protestant, explained her thoughts about her niece who came out: "I've got a great niece who has just said that she thinks she's gay. I don't exactly like the comment that 'I am gay' because I don't think she knows what she is right now. I think she's confused, you know. And I feel like what it is is gay tendencies, those kinds of things." Why would a person want to come out to their family only to be shunned or doubted? It is already extremely difficult to build up the courage to tell a loved one that you are gay, especially when you know they believe your sexuality is sinful. Imagine, after building up the courage to come out and all the emotional labor that entails, being told you do not know what you are talking about and that you merely have "gay tendencies." This is one reason social contact is often limited between gay and lesbian people and Mississippi Christians.

Another evangelical Protestant, Frances, relayed a story similar to Erica's. Frances has a son who is gay, and she explained that she does not accept his "lifestyle" and chose not to tell people when he came out to her. I asked Frances if she was embarrassed to tell people, and she clarified:

I wouldn't say embarrassed. No. There was a different reason I didn't want to tell them; it wasn't because of embarrassment. . . . Because my thought was . . . he has gone through school being called gay because he didn't participate in sports, and then so many years of being called that I guess you get to the point where you believe it like everything else. . . . I say he's confused, and I didn't want to tell any and everybody and have it be out there and then when he comes to the realization of . . . the life that he's supposed to live, then he'd have to go back and, you know, face these people . . . when they assume he's one thing and he's not. You understand what I'm saying? . . . It's out of protection.

Clearly, this respondent felt her son's sexuality was just a phase, something he would move past. These respondents felt that their friends or family members simply needed help realizing they were not actually gay.

Due to the real and perceived threats of coming out to Christian friends and family members, many gay and lesbian people chose not to take the risk. In fact, most interviewees explained that their family member or friend never came out to them, but many interviewees felt that they "just knew" their friend or family member was gay or lesbian. Again, respondents often conflated gender and sexuality; if a boy or man does not act masculine enough, or a girl or woman feminine enough, then many interviewees explained this was a sure sign they were gay or lesbian. For instance, Angela, an evangelical Protestant, told me she always knew her nephew was gay. She stated, "He just kind of grew up that way, acting sissy or whatever, and so we just all kind of always assumed he was like that [gay] . . . Not really sissy, he just always was—you know, he wanted to bake and he wanted to act and he wanted to . . . Anyway, I don't know, his mannerisms just always seemed very not manly. Feminine, yeah." Based on gender expression alone, some respondents made assumptions about a friend's or relative's sexuality.

In a similar example, Ervin, an evangelical Protestant, told me that he knows his nephew is gay even though he has not come out: "I don't think he's admitted it yet. He hasn't come out and publicly said it . . . [but] there's little doubt. . . . I'm just saying that, um, all of his friends, like, most of his friends, are [gay] . . . and his mannerisms and activities and everything else, so it's something that I've, you know, pretty much seen." In this case, the assumption of being gay is based on "mannerisms and activities." Additionally, Ervin added that if a person has mostly gay friends, then it can be assumed that they are also gay, implying that gay people would mostly hang out with other gay people.

These assumptions could mean that some of the reported relationships with gay and lesbian people may only be perceived; the friend or family member may not actually identify as gay or lesbian. This is also important because this study takes place in the Deep South, where what it means to be a "real man" is much more limited than what it means in, say, New York City. In the Deep South, manhood is often measured by stereotypically masculine behaviors such as hunting, shooting guns, driving a big truck, not caring about your appearance, and playing sports. Not living up to these hegemonic stereotypes or norms could lead to being labeled gay even if you are not. For instance, Frances said that her son eventually accepted the label of gay after being called this for years because he was not interested in sports.

This labeling also occurs with lesbians, but the descriptions differ. Girls and women are allowed more fluidity in their presentation of gender than boys and men are. Doing stereotypically masculine things, such as playing sports, does not necessary mean that a girl or woman is a lesbian. Yet even this did not stop some respondents from making assumptions about their friends' or relatives' sexuality. Deborah, a forty-five-year-old white mainline Protestant from northeast Mississippi, explained that her aunt did not have to come out to her because Deborah already knew she was a lesbian. She said, "I knew she was gay before she knew she was gay. . . . She didn't tell me; she doesn't have to tell me." Deborah was confident in her ability to discern her aunt's sexuality without ever being told, but she did not go into detail on how she was able to gather this information.

When I asked interviewees if they were embarrassed by their gay or lesbian friends or relatives, a handful indicated they were not embarrassed, but their justifications for this response painted a different picture. To prove their lack of embarrassment, some interviewees used examples of asking others to pray for them or bringing them along to church. For instance, Angela explained that she was not embarrassed by her nephew, who identifies as gay: "In fact, I brought his name up to my Sunday school class and asked them to pray for him and all." Thus, even though respondents indicated that they did not feel embarrassed, it is worth noting that they only presented them to other Christians in the context of asking for help to "fix" them while implicitly claiming heterosexual privilege for themselves.

Finally, many interviewees tried to explain why they were not close to their gay and lesbian friends and family members. Although some of the reasons seem unrelated to sexual orientation, others appeared to be justifications for no longer wanting to spend time with friends or family members after discovering their sexuality. Lack of closeness was often explained away by distance, age, change in interest, and children. For example, Caleb, an evangelical Protestant, told me that he used to be very close to his wife's cousin who is gay. He said they were no longer close but that it was not due to his sexuality. Caleb explained, "It doesn't affect our relationship um, the fact that he's gay, it's more that our interests have changed." However, when Caleb described how their interests have changed, the changes all revolved around sexuality. For example, he explained that now his wife's cousin is very "promiscuous" and likes "go-go dancing or whatever in clubs." He said they can no longer hold conversations because they have nothing in common, but that they both still like to play games together. It seems from his answer that the lack of closeness is directly related to sexuality, although he described these things as interests.

The Influence of Having a Gay or Lesbian Friend or Family Member

A major goal of this study is to determine whether having a friend or relative who identifies as gay or lesbian influences Christians' beliefs about homosexuality and gay and lesbian rights. So far, I have examined Mississippi Christians' religious beliefs, their attitudes toward gay and lesbian rights, and their social contact with gay and lesbian people. Here I demonstrate how respondents' relationships with gay and lesbian people influence their beliefs and attitudes about homosexuality and gay and lesbian rights. I asked interviewees if they felt that their relationships with gay and lesbian people had changed their views on how Christians should approach homosexuality and gay and lesbian rights. While individual answers varied widely, a general pattern emerged. To understand the influence (or lack thereof) of this social contact, I discuss responses in four theoretical categories: "A Case for Coming Out," "Allies and Friends," "Love the Sinner, Hate the Sin," and "Homosexuality Is an Abomination."

Figure 1 illustrates the intersections between the belief that having a gay or lesbian friend or family member influenced attitudes toward gay and lesbian civil rights and interviewees' actual support or opposition to gay and lesbian rights. For example, the respondents in the "A Case for Coming Out" category felt that having a gay or lesbian friend or family member positively influenced their beliefs about gay and lesbian rights *and* held beliefs that were either fully or conditionally supportive of gay and lesbian rights. On the contrary, the respondents in the "Homosexuality Is an Abomination" category stated that having a gay or lesbian friend or family member did not influence their beliefs about gay and lesbian rights, *and* they continued to completely oppose or only conditionally support gay and lesbian rights. Figure 2 illustrates how these four categories are distributed through the three religious categories in this study—mainline Protestants, Catholics, and evangelical Protestants. I explain each category in turn and provide examples from the interviewees.

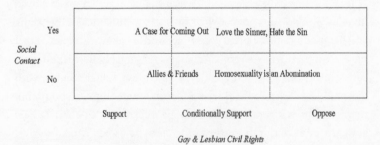

FIG. 1. The Influence of Having a Gay or Lesbian Friend or Family Member on the Acceptance of Gay and Lesbian Civil Rights

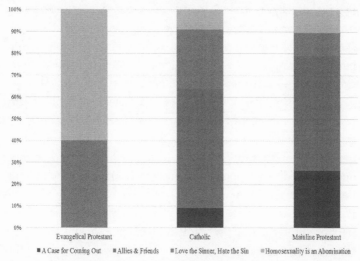

FIG. 2. The Influence of Having a Gay or Lesbian Friend or Family Member by Religious Category

A CASE FOR COMING OUT

Responses that fell into the "A Case for Coming Out" category fit the expected outcomes of social contact—that is, the respondents in this category validated Allport's (1954) and Pettigrew's (1998) theory that if people from different groups get to know each other, this will encourage more accurate and positive beliefs and attitudes across groups. As negative stereotypes about a group decrease, so do prejudice and discrimination. The respondents in this category described holding conservative and often-stereotypical beliefs about homosexuality and gay and lesbian rights prior to knowing that a friend or family member identified as gay or lesbian. After personally getting to know someone who identified as gay or lesbian, these interviewees moved to fully supporting gay and lesbian rights. Additionally, these respondents either no longer felt that homosexuality was sinful or felt that it was at least not an issue on which they should pass judgment.

Overall, six of the forty interviewees fit into this description; five of these respondents identified as mainline Protestants, and one identified as Catholic. They all indicated that getting to know someone who identified as gay or lesbian changed their beliefs about gay and lesbian rights; all six of these interviewees fully supported same-sex marriage and adoption. Notably, no evangelical Protestants were steered to full acceptance of homosexuality and gay and lesbian civil rights as a result of having a friend or family member who identified as gay or lesbian. Social contact with gay and lesbian people clearly had the greatest positive impact on mainline Protestants, who indicated that it led them to be more open-minded and supportive of gay and lesbian rights. While my findings support Bramlett's (2012) assertion that social contact is not sufficient for white evangelical Protestants, at least in Mississippi, the results of my study contradict her claim that social contact does not have positive influences on white mainline Protestants' beliefs about same-sex marriage and instead show that it was white mainline Protestants who were most greatly influenced by social contact with gay and lesbian individuals. All six of the respondents who believed that social contact changed their views about gay and lesbian rights identified as white, and five of the six identified as mainline Protestant.

If my own family had been a part of this study, the majority of my family members would also fall into this category. My mother, sister, grandmother, and a number of other family members spent their entire lives in a mainline Protestant (United Methodist) church. Each held stereotypes and misconceptions about being gay or lesbian. Prior to my coming out, I am sure the majority of them would have voted against initiatives for gay and lesbian civil rights, including same-sex marriage and adoption. My coming out changed this; over time, my family has come to be more accepting and supportive of gay and lesbian equality, largely because they understand how these decisions influence my life.

In a similar manner, Kelsey, a mainline Protestant, provided an excellent example of opinions held by those in the group "A Case for Coming Out." She explained how her views had shifted after getting to know gay and lesbian people and how she believed that social contact could change Christians' views more generally. She stated:

> In high school, I was hanging out with some more conservative Christians, that's a nice way to put it . . . and the more I got to know [gay and lesbian] people and know their stories and figure out what was important, and also the more I thought about the political side of it and all that, it changed my mind. . . . It's not a personal struggle for me. It's easy for me to get married, which I also feel guilty about. . . . Because I have the privilege, I guess it's something like white privilege, you know, or hetero privilege or whatever. . . . But once getting to know [gay and lesbian] people, I think that [change] went across the board. . . . I think [getting to know gay and lesbian people] will wake up Christians across the board.

As this quote illustrates, these shifts in attitudes and beliefs were not immediate, but over time, people in this category began to think about the rights they were entitled to and examine inequality. After personally getting to know someone who is gay or lesbian, people in this group began to question whether they could deny these friends and family members the same rights they had been granted. These respondents believed that getting to know gay and lesbian people should have a positive influence on Christians in general and lead to a reduction in prejudice.

Similar to Kelsey, Gretchen, a seventy-year-old white mainline Protestant in northeast Mississippi, felt that getting to know gay and lesbian people should have the ability to open Christians' hearts and minds and help them make their religious beliefs more accepting. Gretchen explained, "I don't know how anyone could be prejudiced about a group of people without knowing the group of people. And I bet the people who are prejudiced about [homosexuality and gay and lesbian civil rights] don't open their hearts or their minds to knowing someone gay or lesbian, or bisexual. . . . I have a problem with that part of the faith of some of the religions."

Gretchen could not understand how some religious denominations or individuals could continue to hold prejudicial attitudes toward gay and lesbian people after getting to know someone who identified this way. Yet many respondents were not ready or willing to open their minds when it came to issues of sexuality.

ALLIES AND FRIENDS

Within the gay and lesbian civil rights movement, "ally" is often used to refer to heterosexual people who support and fight for LGBTQ rights. In this study, sixteen of the forty interviewees explained that social contact did not influence their views about homosexuality and gay and lesbian civil rights because they had never judged gay and lesbian people. Some of the respondents in this category suggested that social contact did not change their beliefs per se, because they had not formed any beliefs prior to contact. As more and more individuals get to know gay and lesbian people, and as our society becomes more open about sexuality, the category "Allies and Friends" will most likely contain the majority of Americans. Most children and young adults today have always known someone who identifies as gay or lesbian. People are also exposed to gay and lesbian characters on television and in movies at a far higher rate than in the past (Gross 2001; Hart 2000). As this trend continues, it will be more difficult to determine if social contact really influences beliefs and attitudes. The fact that no one in this category fully opposed same-sex marriage or adoption, however, likely indicates that having a gay or lesbian friend or relative did have a positive influence on beliefs and attitudes toward homosexuality and gay and lesbian rights. Nevertheless, because the respondents in this category do not remember a time before having contact or being open-minded about issues of sexuality, it is hard to determine which came first—contact or beliefs.

Of the "Allies and Friends" in this study, ten identified as mainline Protestants, and six identified as Catholics. (Not surprisingly, no evangelical Protestants suggested they had always supported gay and lesbian civil rights or always known someone who identified as gay or lesbian.) The majority of the respondents in this category fully accepted gay and lesbian rights, although some continued to hold reservations concerning certain rights. Twelve of the sixteen "Allies and Friends" supported same-sex marriage, while the remaining four suggested they supported equal rights but not marriage for same-sex couples. Similarly, eleven of the sixteen fully supported same-sex adoption, while five offered conditional support but continued to feel that same-sex adoption was not ideal for children.

Brenda, a Catholic respondent who conditionally supported gay and lesbian rights, explained that relationships with gay and lesbian people had not influenced her beliefs and attitudes toward homosexuality and gay and lesbian rights because she had always been open-minded and accepting. She said, "I grew up in a household that was very . . . understanding of different cultures and respectful of different opinions as long as it wasn't infringing on someone's rights, so I don't know that [social contact] really shaped [my opinions] necessarily. I think I already had the inherent perspective and appreciation for different values from my home life, maybe not really for gay and lesbian people specifically, but just in general." Social contact was not a necessary factor for change for Brenda. Along the same lines, Tracy, another Catholic who conditionally accepted gay and lesbian rights, explained that social contact did not influence her beliefs because she "never harbored any real prejudices."

Other respondents in this category could not remember a time before they had a friend or family member who identified as gay or lesbian. For instance, Deborah, a mainline Protestant, described, "I was twelve years old . . . the first time I realized [I knew someone who was gay], and I never thought of anything [before]. When you're twelve years old, you don't think about things like that, you think about going and playing." Another mainline Protestant, Nancy, felt that she had never been given the opportunity to form beliefs about the topic before she got to know someone who identified as gay: "You know, I was just so protected as a kid, and so are my children, so what you don't see . . . does not affect you. And I don't think I ever really thought too much about it." Whether it was an open mind or the first time they had considered the topic, these respondents felt that knowing someone who is gay or lesbian was not necessary for their acceptance of equal rights.

LOVE THE SINNER, HATE THE SIN

The respondents in the "Love the Sinner, Hate the Sin" category believed that having a gay or lesbian friend or family member did have a positive impact on their beliefs but still did not fully change their beliefs. The respondents in this category described feeling more sympathetic toward gay and lesbian people after getting to know someone who identified this way, but they continued to be either fully opposed or only conditionally supportive of gay and lesbian civil rights. While those in the "A Case for Coming Out" category aligned their statements of change with belief and action, the respondents in the "Love the Sinner, Hate the Sin" group felt that social contact influenced them, but their responses to other questions did not fully support this assertion. Thus while these interviewees lend some credibility to social contact theory, social contact was not enough to lead them to fully support gay and lesbian equality. The respondents in this category were more likely to weigh their religious identity above their identity as a friend or family member of a gay or lesbian person. These respondents held their religious identity as their master status.[3] By holding a conservative religious identity as a master status, these individuals were unable to fully reap the benefits of social contact with gay and lesbian people. None of the respondents in this category were able to fully support same-sex marriage and adoption, despite their general agreement that having a gay or lesbian friend or relative had a positive influence on their beliefs and attitudes.

In total, four evangelical Protestants, two mainline Protestants, and three Catholics fit this description. The respondents in the "Love the Sinner, Hate the Sin" category generally held more conservative beliefs about being gay or lesbian, and these beliefs continued to outweigh the positive influences of social contact. For example, these interviewees continued to believe that homosexuality was sinful or "unnatural," and they continued to oppose or only conditionally support gay and lesbian civil rights. Four of the respondents in this group completely opposed same-sex marriage, four supported civil unions but not marriage, and only one supported same-sex marriage. When it came to same-sex adoption, two were completely opposed, five argued it was not ideal, and two supported it. Despite these stances on gay and lesbian rights, these interviewees felt that social contact successfully reduced negative attitudes toward gay and lesbian people. Respondents in this group indicated that they had learned how to approach the subject more from a "place of love" after getting to know someone who identified as gay or lesbian. These respondents align with Lewis's (2011) findings that social contact had some positive benefits for conservative Christians, albeit benefits weaker than those seen in other groups.

Candace, an evangelical Protestant, explained how getting to know gay and lesbian people had helped her, although she continued to feel strongly that homosexuality was sinful: "Hopefully people react with the fact when talking to someone who's walking in that lifestyle, they're talking to a human being, you know, and show respect for that person as a human being. But also, reach out to them in a way that you know they can be helpful in some way." Through interaction with gay and lesbian people, Candace decided that gay and lesbian people must be approached as human beings deserving of respect, but for Candace, respect did not include acceptance or a change in her beliefs and attitudes about homosexuality. For her, respect for gay and lesbian people entailed helping them see the error of their ways and turn away from what she saw as a sinful "lifestyle." In Candace's eyes, approaching gay and lesbian people with respect meant helping them see sexuality in the same way that she does: based in biblical literalism.

Susan, a Catholic respondent, also fit into the "Love the Sinner, Hate the Sin" category. When I asked her if getting to know someone who identified as gay or lesbian had changed her opinion of gay and lesbian rights, she said, "Probably. I probably didn't even think they should have civil unions. . . . It's mellowed me a bit." Once more, the positive influences expected from knowing someone of another group were present, but conservative religious beliefs continued to temper acceptance of gay and lesbian rights. This could still be seen as a win for gay and lesbian equality: at least conservative Christians are arguing for open arms and see gay and lesbian people as humans. Yet simply acknowledging another person's humanity is not the leap in consciousness needed to effect tangible change in the lives of gay and lesbian people in the United States.

The "Love the Sinner, Hate the Sin" category neither negated nor bolstered previous research on social contact. What it did show was that in order to bring about equality, another strategy is needed in place of or in addition to simply getting to know gay and lesbian people. Hillary's story provides a vivid illustration of why this matters. While social contact had a positive influence on Hillary's beliefs and attitudes toward homosexuality, she still struggled to overcome the dissonance between her conservative Catholic beliefs and loving her brother, who identifies as gay. As previously indicated, many Catholics in this study inhabited the middle ground between acceptance and condemnation; they displayed higher levels of ambivalence than either evangelical or mainline Protestants. These Mississippi Catholics often struggled to reconcile the discord between what church doctrine says about homosexuality and their relationships with gay and lesbian people.

Hillary, a white woman in her midfifties, displayed the ambivalence and dissonance some conservative Catholics face. While social contact had a positive influence on her beliefs and attitudes toward homosexuality and gay and lesbian civil rights, it had not had a strong enough influence to change her conservative religious beliefs about the topic. Prior to learning that her brother was gay, Hillary was secure in her belief that homosexuality is wrong and sinful. She explained, "Before my brother had his out-of-the-closet experience to us, I thought homosexuality was wrong. You know, all the verses in the Bible points toward [homosexuality] being wrong. But then when my brother announced that he was gay, I guess it really made me think about what I was reading. And if I truly am a Catholic, and I truly believe the catechism, the catechism teaches that homosexuality is wrong. But the thing that just keeps coming back in my mind is that our God is a God of love, and when in doubt, love." She continued by explaining that she prayed to God and asked God why the Bible is not clearer on the issue of homosexuality. She sought a straightforward answer, and in its absence, she clung to the idea of love. Still, even this solution did not set Hillary at ease because she believed the true interpretation of the Bible is found in the catechism, which condemns homosexuality. She found it extremely difficult to merge her religious beliefs and her love for her brother. Her ambivalence became even clearer when I asked if she agreed with the Catholic Church's teachings on homosexuality. She responded, "Yes. Yes. Do I sound like I do based on the answers that I give? Or am I on the fence?" Even in an interview about her beliefs, she was seeking answers; she wanted me, the interviewer, to help clarify her dissonance and uneasiness about her beliefs.

Hillary went on to explain how learning that her brother was gay changed her opinion about homosexuality being a choice. She said that she knew her brother did not choose to be gay: "I used to think that it was chosen, a chosen way of life, but I know with my brother, it was not, because even when he was little he had female tendencies. . . . I know he didn't choose that way of life . . . but that's just the way God made him." She described this as her "dilemma": How could she condemn someone if he was the way God made him? So social contact did have some positive benefits for Hillary. For one, her shift in belief about the nature of homosexuality is an important, as research shows that people who believe homosexuality is a choice are much more likely to believe it is a sin and to vote against gay and lesbian rights. Nevertheless, when I asked Hillary if gay and lesbian people should be allowed to marry, she answered, "I don't know. Now I mean, there's a part of me that says no, that it does not lead to a good family life. But yet, you know, how can [gay and lesbian people] be denied the wonderful gift of a family?" Ultimately, she explained that gay and lesbian people getting married would devalue the institution of marriage, and she believed civil unions would be a better option instead: "I like the idea of keeping it a civil union. . . . I think it comes down to defining what is a marriage, and most churches define marriage as between a man and a woman. So, let's not get that confused. Let's not expand that definition. Instead, let's make a new word for it."

Similarly, when it came to the issue of same-sex adoption, Hillary was "on the fence." She argued that same-sex couples raising children was not an ideal situation but that it was better than children not having parents at all. Despite her brother—whom she loved dearly—being gay and her change of heart about homosexuality being a choice, she still could not adapt her religious beliefs to fully support equality for gay and lesbian people. She wanted her brother to be happy but felt the need to put new labels and conditions on the rights he could be granted.

Overall, Hillary believed that her brother coming out to her had positively influenced their relationship. She stated that she now felt closer to him, but she still felt somewhat embarrassed by his sexual orientation. For instance, she explained that she did not feel comfortable telling her children that her brother is gay. Despite these reservations, Hillary did feel that knowing her brother is gay had changed the way she saw homosexuality and gay and lesbian rights. She was now more "lenient" about civil rights than she had been before she knew about her brother's sexuality. Additionally, she told me that as a Christian, she focused more on love now than on the prohibitions against homosexuality.

In each of the previous cases, social contact had at least some positive impact on respondents' beliefs and attitudes about homosexuality and gay and lesbian rights. While some interviewees continued to hold the same beliefs after getting to know someone who identifies as gay or lesbian, they at least felt that they were more respectful of gay and lesbian people after social contact. Others, like Hillary, continued to feel extreme dissonance and uncertainty about how to align their religious beliefs with their relationships with gay and lesbian people. These feelings of uncertainty appeared to be most common among Mississippi Catholics who cared deeply about someone who is gay or lesbian but could not find a place within their faith that would allow them to be completely accepting of homosexuality.

HOMOSEXUALITY IS AN ABOMINATION

The final category of respondents, "Homosexuality Is an Abomination," continued to reject homosexuality and gay and lesbian civil rights even after getting to know someone who identified as gay or lesbian. This group brings to light a gap in the social contact literature: How can a person know—and even love—someone who identifies as gay or lesbian yet continue to hold stereotypical and prejudicial views about them? The interviewees in this category maintained that homosexuality is always sinful, and they continued to be fully opposed to or only conditionally support gay and lesbian rights. Continuing to reject homosexuality after getting to know someone who is gay or lesbian suggests that conservative religion is a negative feature that deters the positive benefits of social contact. When respondents' religious identities were their primary identity, or master status, knowing someone who is gay or lesbian had no apparent influence on their beliefs about homosexuality. These respondents were in no way ambivalent or confused about their beliefs; they were certain their religious convictions were correct and that gay and lesbian people needed to hear the "truth" in order to be set free. As the adage goes, these respondents were determined to "pray the gay away"; they could not accept homosexuality while continuing to identify as Christians. To the respondents in this category, accepting homosexuality and gay and lesbian rights meant rejecting their religious beliefs at least to some degree.

The respondents in the "Homosexuality Is an Abomination" category best fit Smith et al.'s (1998) theory of subcultural identity. Despite social contact with gay and lesbian people, these respondents felt the need to police the boundaries of their faith from those who "choose that kind of lifestyle." These interviewees felt embattled by the perceived immoral forces of secular society, which to them included homosexuality. Their fears provided intense motivation to keep gay and lesbian people from obtaining the same rights and privileges these respondents held. Members of this category clearly demonstrated the idea of distinction-with-engagement (Smith et al. 1998). These Christians strongly and clearly distinguished themselves from gay and lesbian people and distinguished their institutional forms of marriage and child rearing from "nontraditional" family forms. The respondents in the "Homosexuality Is an Abomination" category did not ignore the issue of gay and lesbian civil rights; on the contrary, they felt called by their religion and God to engage with activists and gay and lesbian people in order to change their sexuality and stance on issues of gay and lesbian equality.

In total, nine of the forty interviewees said that relationships with gay or lesbian people did not change their attitudes or beliefs about homosexuality and gay and lesbian rights. Of the nine respondents in the "Homosexuality Is an Abomination" category, six were evangelical Protestants,[4] two were mainline Protestants, and one was Catholic. Erica, an evangelical Protestant, explained the sentiment of those in this category clearly: "I always kind of felt like whether I knew people or not, [homosexuality] was wrong and it shouldn't be happening. So, I don't think [my views] changed just because I got to know people that are [gay or lesbian]." Similarly, another evangelical Protestant, Darlene, discussed how having a close friend in high school who was gay did not make her more accepting of homosexuality and gay and lesbian rights:

It did make it hard, because I would never try to come at him that he was wrong. But I still, as a Christian, I think that Jesus offers us a lot of good things, and I wouldn't want [my friend] not to know that. But he was always uncomfortable with [discussing religion] because of his lifestyle, and he knew that the church doesn't necessarily uphold that. Most of them [gay and lesbian people] as a whole don't [want to talk about it], and so he kind of just got quiet and would just change the subject type of thing if that ever came up, like religious beliefs and stuff.

Darlene's religious identity and beliefs were more important to her than her identity as a friend to someone who identified as gay. While she tried to be considerate of him, she felt it was important to tell him her beliefs. As Candace described earlier, people need to be respectful, but at the same time, some feel a Christian duty to help gay and lesbian people recognize what they are doing is wrong.

Along the same lines, Ervin also held conservative religious beliefs despite the fact that he attended a mainline Protestant church. He was one of two mainline Protestants who rejected homosexuality completely even after getting to know someone who identified as gay or lesbian. Ervin had a nephew who identified as gay and a niece who identified as lesbian. Despite having a close relationship with his gay and lesbian family members, he strongly believed that churches should only accept gay and lesbian people in order to help them change. He explained, "You have to say everything about this particular behavior [homosexuality] is unacceptable. . . . If you say this behavior is acceptable, your religion means pretty much nothing, if you simply accept everything that's going on out there." Social contact had no impact on Ervin's beliefs; even with close relatives who identify as gay and lesbian, he still believed that everything about homosexuality is immoral.

Another exemplar of this category was Frances, an evangelical Protestant. Her story demonstrated a clear example of religious identity outweighing the positive benefits of having a gay or lesbian family member. Approximately seven years ago, when her son was eighteen years old, he came out to her as gay. Despite extremely close social contact, she continued to believe that homosexuality is always sinful; she said it is simply "not God's way." Seven years later, Frances continued to fully oppose gay and lesbian rights. She maintained that same-sex marriage would add to the "downward spiral" of marriage and that she would also not support civil unions for same-sex couples. When it came to same-sex adoption, Frances believed that other people would be cruel to the children of same-sex parents and that same-sex adoption would lead to confusion for children.

Frances described a close relationship with her son before finding out he was gay, yet she did not feel that their currently strained relationship was a result of her beliefs and attitudes about homosexuality and gay and lesbian rights. She explained, "[We are] not as close as we used to be, and it has nothing to do with his lifestyle." However, as she continued, it became clear that her son's sexuality was indeed a barrier in their relationship. When I asked if her son's sexuality affected their relationship, she stated, "As far as he's concerned it did. . . . Because I don't believe what he believes in. He felt distant. . . . He was upset because I didn't accept it. So, I mean it's gotten better, our relationship, but it's not the way it was."

It was clear Frances loved her son, but social contact was not enough to change her conservative religious beliefs about homosexuality or to justify support of gay and lesbian rights. Frances hoped her son would recognize that homosexuality is sinful and that he was merely reacting to the social conditions of the bullying he faced in high school. She told me that her son's sexuality in no way changed her beliefs about gay and lesbian civil rights or how Christians should deal with the issue of homosexuality. She said, "He knows, I feel like . . . the life he leads is not according to the Bible, and he knows that I don't believe in it." Frances did not think her religious beliefs should be questioned; it was her son who was confused, not her. In her mind, her son was struggling because of his own choice to be gay, not because his mother had rejected him.

In all the instances in the "Homosexuality Is an Abomination" category, social contact failed to have the positive influences expected. Conservative religious beliefs persisted in this category, despite having gay or lesbian friends or relatives. These Mississippi Christians strongly believed that caring for their friend or family member meant showing, through their actions, what it means to be a Christian and hoping friends and family members would eventually recognize their sins and repent.

* * * * *

Overall, it is clear that social contact is not always enough to overcome prejudice. So what do these theoretical categories reveal about the impacts of social contact with gay and lesbian people? The main takeaway of this study is that evangelical Protestantism generally negates the positive benefits of social contact with gay and lesbian people. While getting to know a gay or lesbian person led some evangelical Protestants to be more sympathetic, it did not influence their belief that homosexuality is a sin. Additionally, having a friend or family member who identified as gay or lesbian was not enough to lead any evangelical Protestants to fully support gay and lesbian rights.

The only respondents who completely shifted their beliefs about homosexuality and gay and lesbian rights were five mainline Protestants and one Catholic. Five of the nineteen mainline Protestants in this study indicated they previously held negative beliefs about homosexuality and did not support gay and lesbian rights. Yet after getting to know someone who identifies as gay or lesbian, these respondents changed their perspectives. In addition to the five respondents who changed their beliefs, six of the mainline Protestant respondents indicated they had always accepted gay and lesbian people. Only four mainline Protestants held homosexuality to be sinful or were opposed to at least some gay and lesbian rights after getting to know someone who is gay or lesbian.

Catholics' beliefs were less predictable in this study; these respondents usually took more of a middle ground on issues of homosexuality and gay and lesbian rights than evangelical Protestants and mainline Protestants. Only one Catholic continued to believe that homosexuality is always a sin and continued to oppose the majority of gay and lesbian rights after social contact. On the other end of the spectrum, only one Catholic suggested that social contact changed their views completely and that they now fully supported same-sex marriage and adoption. The majority of Catholics indicated that having a gay or lesbian friend or family member made them more understanding (but did not lead to a complete shift in beliefs) or that homosexuality and gay and lesbian rights were not issues they had considered before getting to know someone who identified this way.

This means that social contact may not be the golden ticket to overcoming prejudice and discrimination that we have long hoped it would be. While getting to know gay and lesbian people has a positive influence on mainline Protestants and more liberal Catholics, it does not appear to be as beneficial for conservative Christians. Despite the many positive benefits of social contact between groups, Pettigrew and Tropp (2006) are correct that there are negative features that deter the positive benefits of social contact. Conservative religion is one of these negative features.

Despite having friends and family members who are gay or lesbian, evangelical Protestants and conservative Catholics in Mississippi continued to believe that homosexuality is sinful and that gay and lesbian people should attempt to overcome this sin. Conservative Christians' religious identity appears to be more important than their relationships with gay and lesbian people. The need for a subcultural identity to set them apart from the rest of society seems to outweigh the positive benefits of social contact with gay and lesbian people. Conservative Christians either weigh their religious identity more heavily than their relationships with gay and lesbian friends and family members or accept the cognitive dissonance[5] that comes with maintaining close social contact with gay and lesbian people while simultaneously believing in a religion that condemns homosexuality.

Christians may be torn between supporting their loved ones and adhering to a religion that is extremely important to them. While this dichotomy did not lead to cognitive dissonance for all respondents, some interviewees—especially conservative Catholics—expressed sincere discomfort and struggled with merging these two realities. On the other hand, some respondents admitted they had not even considered there was a discord between their beliefs and behaviors before speaking to me. Some chose to keep the two things separate: they had gay and lesbian friends, and they went to a church that condemned their friends' sexuality—they did not perceive these positions as contradictory. Others believed the only way to show compassion to their gay and lesbian friends and family members was by trying to help them see the error of their ways. They felt that loving someone who is gay or lesbian meant changing *them* rather than changing their own beliefs.

In conclusion, the positive benefits of having gay or lesbian friends or family members were only evident with mainline Protestants and some Catholics. These respondents focused on biblical passages about love and being nonjudgmental. They ignored or reinterpreted passages others used to show that homosexuality is sinful, and they felt their loved ones were more important than a few biblical passages interpreted by some to condemn homosexuality. Getting to know someone who identified as gay or lesbian had the ability to override prejudice and lead to support of gay and lesbian rights for those who did not hold conservative religious beliefs.

For those who placed their conservative religious identity at the forefront, social contact was not sufficient for overcoming prejudice. Their subcultural identity (Smith et al. 1998) as Christians was more important than their relationships with gay and lesbian people. Although it is beyond the scope of this study to determine if there are other ways to overcome prejudice and opposition to gay and lesbian civil rights, opportunities appear slim. If having a gay or lesbian child or sibling could not override conservative Christians' negative beliefs about homosexuality, what will? Hopefully, circumstances are not as bleak as one mainline Protestant put it: "I believe that for your generation and my son's generation [millennials], [homosexuality] is not even an issue. And I think it will ultimately change, but I think there will need to be a few more funerals." When I asked him to expand, he continued: "People of my generation and older need to die."

Conclusion

When Religion Overshadows Relationships

To me, the grounds for hope are simply that we don't know what will
happen next, and that the unlikely and the unimaginable transpire quite
regularly. And that the unofficial history of the world shows that dedicated
individuals and popular movements can shape history and have, though
how and when we might win how long it takes is not predictable.
—Rebecca Solnit (2014, 87–88)

The study provides a more complete understanding of Christians'
beliefs and attitudes toward homosexuality and gay and lesbian
civil rights and the influence of having a gay or lesbian friend
or family member on these beliefs and attitudes. Through interviews with forty Mississippi Christians, I examined what Christians believe about homosexuality, whether Christians support or
oppose rights for gay and lesbian people, and how Christians make
sense of their relationships with friends and relatives who identify
as gay or lesbian in light of their religious beliefs. Conservative
Christians are often vocal opponents of gay and lesbian rights in
the United States, but proponents of gay and lesbian civil rights
rarely take the time to listen to their beliefs and fully understand
them. In this book, I provide a more nuanced perspective of Christians' beliefs and what they mean for gay and lesbian rights today.

Understanding how Christianity and relationships with gay
and lesbian people work together or negate one another when
it comes to prejudice and discrimination against gay and lesbian

people provides valuable information for those seeking equality. Mississippi was chosen as the location for this study because of the large proportion of conservative Christians and the state's standing as a place where gay and lesbian rights remain scarce and highly opposed. By learning more about Mississippi Christians' beliefs and attitudes toward homosexuality and gay and lesbian civil rights, activists and proponents of equality can better understand the interactions between Christianity and prejudice and how this is influenced by relationships with gay and lesbian people.

When it comes to beliefs about homosexuality and gay and lesbian rights, the respondents interviewed for this study held varying beliefs and attitudes that ranged from complete rejection and opposition to complete acceptance and support. These beliefs and attitudes varied based on religious affiliation and were far more complex and diverse than suggested by media and research. Many respondents in this study demonstrated uncertainty and contradictory positions when it came to the issues of homosexuality and gay and lesbian rights, especially conservative Catholics. While it could be argued that this ambivalence was used to conceal homophobic beliefs, these respondents genuinely appeared to be torn over how best to address the issues of homosexuality and gay and lesbian rights. The respondents who neither fully supported nor opposed rights seemed to be sincerely grappling with the complex process of aligning their Christian beliefs with their emotional attachments to gay and lesbian people.

In general, evangelical Protestants held the most conservative views about homosexuality. Supporting Smith et al.'s (1998) theory of subcultural identity, evangelical Protestants used the issue of homosexuality to set themselves apart from the national mainstream culture, which seems to them to be moving toward equality. Evangelical Protestants' beliefs about homosexuality and gay and lesbian civil rights created an embattled identity and led them to fight against a society that is, in their opinion, shifting further away from God. This struggle against society provided an important identity marker for evangelical Protestants, and it allowed them to thrive based on their distinction. Evangelical Protestants across the state of Mississippi largely opposed same-sex marriage, same-sex adoption, and the gay and lesbian civil rights movement. They used the issues surrounding gay and lesbian rights as a boundary to protect their embattled Christian identity. They clearly explained that granting gay and lesbian people more rights would be an indication that Christianity, and society more broadly, was heading in a bad direction—away from God's plan. As I argued, although evangelical Protestant opposition did not appear to stem from a place of hatred, opposition to gay and lesbian rights was strong nonetheless.

On a continuum of acceptance of gay and lesbian civil rights, Catholics fell between evangelical and mainline Protestants. In general, Catholics exhibited more ambivalence regarding homosexuality. While they were not fully in line with the larger mainstream culture, Catholics did not appear to be in conflict with society in the same way evangelical Protestants did. When it came to the topic of homosexuality, Catholics leaned more toward acceptance than evangelical Protestants. Still, this acceptance was not complete; they described a conditional inclusion of gay and lesbian people into the Catholic Church and society. Furthermore, Catholics were divided on how to best approach gay and lesbian civil rights. Most Catholics in this study continued to uphold the conservative teachings of the Catholic Church but simultaneously sought to grant gay and lesbian people conditional acceptance in society. In other words, while Catholics felt gay and lesbian people were entitled to rights, they placed conditions on these rights that were not viewed as necessary for heterosexual people. For instance, the Catholics interviewed frequently supported civil unions but not marriage between same-sex partners; supported same-sex adoption but only out of necessity and when certain conditions were met; and were divided over the influence of the gay and lesbian civil rights movement on society.

Mainline Protestants' beliefs about homosexuality aligned more closely with secular society in the United States. Most mainline Protestants in this study argued that homosexuality is not sinful and that the Bible says little or nothing about the issue. Mainline Protestants reasoned that if homosexuality is not sinful, then gay and lesbian people should be accepted fully into their churches and that it is not the place of Christians to judge others' sexuality. These beliefs led most Mainline Protestants to largely support gay and lesbian civil rights. Among respondents, they exhibited the highest levels of support for both same-sex marriage and adoption. Additionally, mainline Protestants generally saw at least some positive benefits of the gay and lesbian civil rights movement.

After understanding respondents' beliefs about homosexuality and gay and lesbian civil rights, I sought to determine if having a gay or lesbian friend or relative had any influence on these beliefs. In chapter 6, I explored the influence of social contact with gay and lesbian people and how Christians reconciled their religious beliefs with their personal relationships with gay and lesbian people. Based on previous research, increased social contact—defined in this study as having a gay or lesbian friend or family member—should have led Mississippi Christians to hold more positive beliefs and attitudes about homosexuality and gay and lesbian rights. On the contrary, this study demonstrates that the positive benefits of social contact were not sufficient for overcoming conservative religious beliefs used to condemn homosexuality. Based on these findings, scholars and activists for equality need to reconsider what leads Christians to oppose gay and lesbian rights and how to properly address this issue.

While the respondents in this study reported relationships with gay or lesbian people, it became clear that conservative religion counterbalanced the potential positive benefits of these connections. Hence conservative religion was a negative feature that deterred the positive influence of social contact from overcoming prejudice. Despite friends and/or family members, evangelical Protestants and conservative Catholics did not change their opinions about the sinful nature of homosexuality, nor did they become more supportive of gay and lesbian rights. While mainline Protestants' and liberal Catholics' beliefs and attitudes toward homosexuality and gay and lesbian rights positively shifted after social contact, conservative Christians held fast to their embattled status and opposition to the cultural mainstream.

Overall, conservative Christians' subcultural identity appeared to be more important than their relationships with gay and lesbian people. Some Catholic respondents did experience cognitive dissonance when trying to live with the contradiction of having gay and lesbian friends and family members while adhering to a religion that they interpreted to condemn homosexuality. On the other hand, most evangelical Protestants did not experience this dissonance; they were confident in their religious beliefs and questioned their friends' or family members' sexuality rather than their own beliefs about homosexuality. Generally, the positive influences of social contact with gay and lesbian people were only evident with mainline Protestants and some Catholics. For conservative Christians, whose religious identity was paramount, social contact was not a sufficient means for overcoming prejudice or to lead to support of gay and lesbian rights; for these respondents, religion overshadowed relationships.

Implications and Why This Matters

First, this research is important because it conclusively shows that religion, specifically conservative Christianity, increases prejudice toward gay and lesbian people (Bramlett 2012; Duck and Hunsberger 1999; Emerson and Smith 2000; Hill et al. 2010; Rowatt et al. 2006). Additionally, this study expands on previous research in order to understand some of the many reasons Christians continue to hold more prejudicial beliefs and attitudes toward homosexuality and gay and lesbian civil rights. Biblical literalism has often been seen as the root of the problem, especially when it comes to the issue of homosexuality, thus leading further investigation to cease. In this book, I demonstrate that it is impossible to gain a true understanding of Christians' beliefs and attitudes toward homosexuality using a simple argument of biblical literalism. While biblical literalism may be a part of the issue, for the Christians in Mississippi to whom I spoke, this issue was far more complex. Many of the respondents in this study did not know what the Bible said about homosexuality, and for the minority who did know, they interpreted it in extremely diverse ways. Those in favor of equality for gay and lesbian people have generally painted a rather limited image of conservative Christians. My conversations with evangelical Protestants and conservative Catholics indicate that their sincere convictions led them to oppose homosexuality and gay and lesbian rights rather than homophobia per se. Many conservative Christians valued their personal relationships with gay and lesbian friends and family members but sometimes struggled to reconcile these relationships with their religious beliefs.

Another important implication of this study is that merely encouraging gay and lesbian people to come out of the closet to conservative Christians will most likely not provide the results desired. At this important stage in the gay and lesbian civil rights movement, proponents of equality must find a new way to approach the vocal minority of conservative Christians who continue to hold strong opposition to gay and lesbian rights. To move forward at this moment in history means to stop painting caricatures of conservative Christians and to listen more fully, and it means acknowledging that coming out to conservative Christians may not provide the positive benefits previously predicted. Now is the time for a new strategy of approaching conservative Christians who oppose gay and lesbian rights. Minimizing conservative Christian beliefs to purely homophobia, hatred, ignorance, and biblical literalism only exacerbates the problem. Conservative Christians do not believe these explanations describe their beliefs, and thus further discussion between conservative Christians and those fighting for gay and lesbian equality is halted. Conservative Christians in this study truly believed the only way to love someone who is gay or lesbian was to help them overcome their sin. By offering a more complete understanding of conservative Christians' beliefs and attitudes toward homosexuality, this study attempts to take a step forward and uncover new approaches to reaching conservative Christians and showing them the harm they are causing to their gay and lesbian friends and family members. These new strategies must allow conservative Christians to hold onto their strong religious identity without limiting the resources and access to equality of their gay and lesbian friends and family members.

Importantly, this study leaves a number of questions to be addressed: What, if anything, can overcome conservative Christians' negative beliefs about homosexuality and lead them toward greater acceptance of gay and lesbian people? What strategies can lead conservative Christians to support gay and lesbian civil rights, not merely conditional inclusion? If close relationships with gay and lesbian people are not enough to overcome stereotypical beliefs, what steps can be taken to ensure equality? The majority of people (87 percent) in the United States already know someone who is gay or lesbian (Drake 2013), and coming out as an approach to overcoming prejudice and bringing about gay and lesbian equality may have reached its limits. Therefore, the potential harm of coming out to conservative Christian may no longer be worth the risks to individual gay and lesbian people.

In a country where "religious freedom" affords people the right to discriminate against LGBTQ people, coming out may no longer be the best solution for overcoming prejudice. Scholars and activists must figure out another way to reach people who are adamant about discriminating against LGBTQ individuals and to alter the perspectives of those who are holding on to a religious conservativism, leading to negative life circumstances for LGBTQ people. For conservative Christians, their master identity is Christian. Therefore, to bring this population to support gay and lesbian equality means making gay and lesbian equality a Christian struggle. It means explaining the benefits of gay and lesbian equality in terms of Christianity and the Bible; no other explanation will be convincing. It means working with and listening to conservative Christian leaders—namely, pastors and priests—who are central to conservative Protestants' and Catholics' understanding of religion and the Bible. If most conservative Christians do not know what the Bible actually says about homosexuality, and they rely on their pastors, priests, and denominations for guidance, activists must work with these leaders to influence change.

Where Do We Go from Here?

While I have provided some suggestions based on my interviews with Mississippi Christians, the magnitude of this dilemma is well beyond the scope of one study. However, there are some basic steps that I see as crucial to dealing with any social problem in our society. First, I wholeheartedly believe that empathy, listening, and understanding must be at the center of a new strategy to move forward. Scholars and activists must stop placing all Christians into one category; there are a large number of Christians who strongly support gay and lesbian rights—even in Mississippi, a state that is often portrayed as being wholly conservative. Mainline Protestants and liberal Catholics in Mississippi appreciated their Christian faith while simultaneously supporting their gay and lesbian friends and family members. They argued that the Bible says little to nothing about homosexuality, and they believed that it is their duty to love others and leave judgment to God.

Additionally, some conservative Catholics strove to align their religious beliefs with their relationships with gay and lesbian people. While they were struggling with this middle ground, their compassion and conditional inclusion could be a guide to reaching others who hold more conservative Christian beliefs. Many times, evangelical Protestants in this study had not considered the dissonance between their religious beliefs and loving someone who is gay or lesbian. Some of these evangelical Protestants acknowledged during their interview that this was the first time they had thought about many of these topics. To me, this suggests that more open and honest conversations are a good place to start; writing off evangelical Protestants as homophobic and hateful will only stop further conversation.

As a sociologist who understands the influence of structure and systemic oppression, I also believe that changing laws and policies surrounding gay and lesbian civil rights may be the most logical way to move forward. While change at the individual level is great, those who support gay and lesbian equality must continue to fight for equal rights under the law. Change in the beliefs and attitudes of conservative Christians will take time, but changing laws and reducing systemic oppression can motivate that change. As seen with interracial marriages in the 1960s, sometimes attitudes must follow changes in law, not vice versa. Historically, conservative Christians held strong opposition to interracial marriages, but since the Supreme Court ruled antimiscegenation laws unconstitutional in 1967, the opposition to interracial marriages has slowly dissipated. As laws change, I am optimistic we will begin to see a change in beliefs and attitudes toward homosexuality and gay and lesbian rights. This can already be seen with the continued uptick in support for same-sex marriage since it became legal across the nation in 2015.

As the African American civil rights movement reminds us, this is not the first time—and likely not the last—that Mississippi will prove to be a key battleground for equality. The higher proportion of conservative people in the state, combined with the importance of conservative Christians' subcultural identities, means that conservative Mississippi Christians will need to continue to build boundaries around their beliefs in order to protect their identities. I am hopeful that the respondent in this study who suggested that society must wait for older generations to die was being overly pessimistic. I agree with Solnit (2014) that there are grounds for hope because we do not know what will happen, and history shows that equality eventually wins. Yet I am more pessimistic about what this means for other groups. Someone will have to replace gay and lesbian people as the "other" for conservative Christians when gay and lesbian people move toward equality. If homosexuality and gay and lesbian rights are no longer the boundary markers of conservative Christians' embattled identity, who will be next? Also, despite movement toward equality, it is evident that African American citizens are still not equal in the state of Mississippi. Although the "wall"—legal barriers to freedom—is no longer being built to keep African American people out per se, a brief look at the news will unmistakably show that African American people are still not seen as first-class citizens in Mississippi.

Today, the political atmosphere in the United States proves that conservatives are intent on maintaining boundaries against the push for equality. The chants to "build a wall" have not dissipated; only where and around whom the wall is being built have changed. Like Hochschild (2016) in her exploration into the conservative political movement in Louisiana, I am not only talking about physical walls or boundaries between groups (although those certainly are a problem); I am also interested in the "empathy walls" that have been erected between conservative and liberal Christians in Mississippi and between conservative Christians and mainstream society more generally. An empathy wall, according to Hochschild (2016), "is an obstacle to deep understanding of another person, one that can make us feel indifferent or even hostile to those who hold different beliefs" (5). Empathy walls are clearly evident in the struggle for gay and lesbian equality.

In the same way religion was intertwined with the African American civil rights movement, a similar story can be told for the gay and lesbian civil rights movement in Mississippi. As Marsh (1997) explains in his book *God's Long Summer*, Mississippians on both sides of civil rights struggles strongly believe that God is on their side. In the struggle for gay and lesbian civil rights, similar patterns emerge as within the African American civil rights movement, where each side identifies with the same religion and Bible yet arrives at a widely different conclusion. Despite some respondents in this study who adamantly disapprove of comparing these two civil rights movements, it is impossible to end this book without pointing out the similarities between these two struggles for equality in Mississippi.

In this book, I ask the reader, as Marsh (1997) did, "to consider how the movement may appear anew if its complex and often cacophonous religious convictions are taken seriously—if the content of such language is not dismissed as smooth justifications of cruelty or dissent, pragmatic tools in the service of political ends, or opiates of the status quo" (3). How do we move beyond seeing conservative Christians' responses to gay and lesbian civil rights as cruel merely for the sake of being cruel? How can we bring Mississippi Christians on both sides of this debate to the table and speak the same language? How can we convince conservative Christians that building more walls will not serve them in the end, especially when these walls are bolstering their identities so completely in the present?

Importantly, we must understand that the story is far more complicated and complex than the media and those outside the state would have us believe. Polarization has led to a standstill. As Hochschild (2016) puts it, "Our polarization, and the increasing reality that we simply don't know each other, makes it too easy to settle for dislike and contempt" (xii). Similarly, in regards to the African American civil rights movement in Mississippi, Marsh (1997) explains that "an accurate picture of how religion shaped the civil rights movement cannot be drawn from a crude juxtaposition of good social gospel guys on the one hand and Bible-thumping racists on the other" (4). Dividing Christians into two groups—those who are loving and nonjudgmental and Bible-thumping homophobes—will not garner the results desired by those striving for equality. We must look more closely at the stories of individuals and how they arrive at their understanding of gay and lesbian civil rights. My hope for this book is that it allows the reader to see the gay and lesbian civil rights movement through the same lens that Marsh (1997) used to explain the African American civil rights movement in Mississippi:

> There are no easy patterns for predicting the way religious ideas govern particular courses of action. Yet there is in each case a theological sense or inner logic in these embodied theologies, and thus there exist patterns specific to the complex interaction of faith and lived experience. I invited the reader to contemplate the inner sense of these religious worlds, to seek an understanding of how the social order looks from the various perspectives of faith, both to broaden our knowledge of the civil rights movement and

better to discern how images of God continue to inform differing visions of civic life and responsibility (4).

By this I mean to invite you, the reader, to find empathy for a position you may not hold or to which you are strongly opposed. I think empathy—putting ourselves in others' shoes and seeing their world from their viewpoint—is the most important characteristic needed for this country to move toward equality. In *Strangers in Their Own Land*, Hochschild (2016) explains, "We, on both sides, wrongly imagine that empathy with the 'other' side brings an end to clearheaded analysis when, in truth, it's on the other side of that [empathy] bridge that the most important analysis can begin" (xi).

If the African American civil rights movement taught us anything, it is that advocates for equality must engage with those holding diametrically opposed worldviews to find common ground. The fight for equality means we are continuously breaking down walls. Yes, new ones are likely to appear, and conservative Christians are continuing to mount barriers to the acceptance of gay and lesbian citizens, as "religious freedom bill" HB 1523 in Mississippi demonstrates. The election of Donald Trump in 2016 and his strong support among Southern evangelical Protestants and conservative Catholics alike have highlighted and even encouraged extreme polarization in the United States. Trump has drawn "a clear dividing line between Christians, to whom he promises the return of Christian public culture" (Hochschild 2016, 224) and Muslims, immigrants, African Americans, gay and lesbian people, and transgender people. While Trump's racism and xenophobia have been largely focused on the politics of race and immigration, his homophobic and transphobic anti-LGBTQ leanings are also clear. His selection of Mike Pence for vice president was a huge victory for anti-LGBTQ conservative Christians. Pence is known for his stance against same-sex marriage, voting against the Employment Non-Discrimination Act, and opposition to LGBTQ people serving openly in the military.

Hochschild (2016) substantiated that "the real function of the excited gathering around Donald Trump is to unify all the white, evangelical enthusiasts who fear that those 'cutting ahead in line' are about to become a terrible, strange, new America" (226). Trump stokes the anxieties of conservative Christians in the United States and reinvigorates looming apprehensions of the "Other." Trump's promises of rescue are empty assurances, but what he does give conservative Christians, especially in the South, "emotionally speaking, is an ecstatic high" (Hochschild 2016, 226). To keep this high, and their embattled and thriving identity, conservative Christians latched on to the divisive rhetoric of Trump. This led them to double-down on the exclusion of others and to refuse to participate in what to them was merely "politically correct speech and ideas" (Hochschild 2016, 227). As Hochschild (2016) shows, in this fight against politically correct attitudes and language, what conservative Christians were really "throwing off" was "a set of *feeling rules*—that is, a set of ideas about the right way to feel regarding blacks, women, immigrants, and gays" (227; emphasis in original).

Those on the political far right that Hochschild (2016) spoke to in Louisiana strongly believed that their version of reality was accurate; hence when those on the political left indicated their version of reality was inaccurate, cruel, and misguided, conservatives felt invalidated, angry, and threatened. Believing their feelings, attitudes, and language were being monitored by liberals, those on the far right—predominantly conservative Christians—rallied behind Trump to have their story heard and take back their "rightful" place in their "own" land. As "religious freedom bills" multiply across the United States and as Trump claims to bring about a Christian resurgence in the country, now more than ever we have to turn off the television and computer to actually hear one another's stories and realities. We must continue to dismantle the walls built to keep African American people, LGBTQ people, and immigrant people out of society and separated from the rights they are entitled to in this country. Yet if we ignore the voices and feelings of those on the other side of the aisle, we will get nowhere. Without empathy, equality is an impossibility.

I hope that this book will continue to prepare Mississippi to move forward, as Marsh (1997) had yearned for more than twenty years ago, and that it will help us move to a time when conservative Christians "will not have to be reminded by the accusing evidence of history that their proclamation has to often served cruel purposes" (Marsh 1997, 8), whether that was their intent or not. I hope that this book can help us progress toward a future where liberal Christians, and the national mainstream culture more generally, will not need to be reminded "that problems will not be solved by hating" conservative Christians (Marsh 1997, 9) or by telling them what to feel (Hochschild 2016). We must now move toward a future where conservative Christians and liberal Christians—the Far Right and the Democratic Socialists, LGBTQ people and people of all colors and genders—"together will reckon with their common humanity" (Marsh 1997, 9).

Appendix

Methodology

To gather my sample of Mississippi Christians, I contacted pastors and priests to ask for permission to recruit members of their congregations. For the initial sample of churches, I compiled a random sample of forty-nine Mississippi churches from the yellow pages. Of the forty-nine churches I contacted to request participation, only three churches agreed to participate in the study. This is telling of the climate in Mississippi for addressing the issue of religion and homosexuality. The majority of churches failed to respond, even after I sent follow-up letters. Five churches declined to participate, one of which sent a note that stated they are a very small church and they "try to go strictly by what the Bible tells us—please mark our church off your list." Due to the low response rate, I relied on snowball sampling to increase my sample size; the three pastors who originally responded were asked if they could recommend other churches that may be willing to participate. From the snowball sampling process, I was able to locate an additional ten churches that were willing to participate, for a total of thirteen churches.

After gathering my sample, I contacted the pastors and priests of the thirteen churches and requested access to their church directories to draw a sample of congregation members. Some pastors and priests did not feel comfortable giving me contact information for their members and opted to distribute the surveys themselves. Of the thirteen churches that agreed to participate, six sent directories, from which I drew a systematic sample of congregation members to survey. I selected the first participant at random then sampled every nth (i.e., eighth) member from the directory. I sent the remaining seven churches a package of thirty surveys to distribute to congregation members of the pastor's or priest's choosing. The churches in the sample consisted of one nondenominational Protestant church, one Lutheran church, seven United Methodist churches, three Catholic churches, one Baptist church, and one Episcopalian church. Protestant churches were divided between evangelical and mainline based on the Pew Forum on Religion and Public Life's (2008) classification of Protestant denominations in the "U.S. Religious Landscape Survey." The United Methodist churches and the Episcopalian church were coded mainline Protestant. The nondenominational Protestant church, the Lutheran church, and the Baptist church are coded as evangelical Protestant.

Although the final sample was not random or necessarily representative of the larger population, the variety of religious backgrounds allowed me to gain a general understanding of Mississippi Christians' beliefs and attitudes toward homosexuality and gay and lesbian civil rights. Additionally, the sample was spread across the state and included both rural and urban areas. Finally, in a state known for conservative politics and religion, I argue that, if anything, my sample will be less conservative than the general population (since respondents were willing to participate in this project). Thus I am more likely to understate rather than overstate the strength of my findings. In a state where almost half of religiously affiliated individuals identify as evangelical Protestants (compared to only 26 percent nationally—see the Pew Forum on Religious and Public Life 2008), I was unable to gather a representative sample of evangelical churches. Only three evangelical churches were willing to participate in this study.

Surveys

I mailed 163 surveys directly to congregation members and 240 for pastors and priests to distribute (403 surveys total) on April 29, 2013. A follow-up letter was sent to individuals on May 30, 2013, and a follow-up email was sent to the pastors and priests to encourage them to distribute the surveys as well as remind their congregations to return them. In order to increase my response rates, I attempted to reduce the costs to respondents by providing addressed, stamped return envelopes and offered an incentive. Respondents were informed in the letter requesting their participation that if they provided their contact information for a potential follow-up interview, they would be entered into a drawing to win one of six $50 gift cards. I mailed the gift cards to six winners on July 12, 2013.

I received a total of 144 completed surveys; a response rate of approximately 36 percent. This response rate is lower than the average of approximately 50 percent for mail surveys that recent research has suggested (Baruch and Holtom 2008; Shih and Fan 2009). Yet it's not surprising considering mailed survey response rates are on the decline (Dey 1997; Sax, Gilmartin, and Bryant 2003). Dey showed the average response rate for national mail surveys had decreased from about 60 percent in the 1960s to about 20 percent by 1997. Based on this finding, my results appear to fall within an acceptable response range.

There are several factors that could have affected my response rate. First, it's clear no individuals from a number of churches (who previously agreed to participate) returned the surveys. One church also informed me the surveys were never distributed which accounts for over 7 percent of failed responses. Another limitation is that some of the addresses in the church directory were outdated (mail was returned and I was unable to find an updated address) and some of the congregation members had passed away or were unable to complete the survey due to health problems (this was noted on returned surveys by the respondents' family member or caretaker) which again lowered my potential sample size. The number of letters returned to me for these reasons were fairly low, only about 2 percent, but I predict others simply threw the letters out rather than returning them.

The survey included questions in four categories: religious beliefs and practices, social contact, social beliefs and attitudes, and demographics. The purpose was to gain an understanding of respondents' religious beliefs and determine how religious affiliation and social contact with gay and lesbian people influenced their beliefs and attitudes about homosexuality and gay and lesbian civil rights.

Interviews

Of the 144 surveys completed, sixty participants provided contact information indicating their willingness to take part in an interview. Fifty-five of these potential interviewees reported social contact with gay or lesbian people. I initially selected thirty-seven potential participants for face-to-face interviews based on the degree of social contact with gay and lesbian family members and friends. All thirty-seven potential interviewees provided contact information and stated in the survey that they had a gay or lesbian friend or family member. I mailed the request letters on August 13, 2013, and potential respondents were asked to choose a location and date that best worked for them. Out of the thirty-seven individuals invited to participate in face-to-face interviews, nineteen individuals signed up by returning the sign-up sheet indicating the location and time most convenient for them. All nineteen individuals who signed up for face-to-face interviews completed the interviews. The interviews were conducted across the state at three different churches, on September 21, September 28, and November 2. The locations were chosen to allow the easiest access for the most respondents—there were locations across the state in south, central, and north Mississippi. The face-to-face interviews were conducted with everyone who signed up, not just the members of the particular churches who allowed me to use their facilities.

After the face-to-face interviews, on November 6, 2013, I sent an additional thirty letters requesting participants sign up for phone interviews. I sent these letters to the eighteen individuals who did not sign up for face-to-face interviews and to an additional twelve individuals. In total, forty-nine survey respondents were asked to participate in an interview. Between November 4 and December 10, I completed twenty-one phone interviews, for a total of forty interviews. As with the surveys, respondents were informed if they participated in the interview they would be entered into a drawing for one of six $50 gift cards. The gift cards were mailed to the six winners on January 8, 2014.

The interview schedule included questions about respondents' religious beliefs and practices, relationships with gay and lesbian people, and social beliefs and attitudes toward homosexuality and gay and lesbian civil rights. During the interviews, I asked respondents open-ended questions and followed up with more specific questions. I designed the interview schedule to gain a more detailed understanding of respondents' relationships with gay and lesbian people and how these relationships did or did not influence their beliefs about homosexuality and gay and lesbian civil rights. Having respondents explain the details of their relationships with gay and lesbian people ("How and when did you meet?" "How did you find out they were gay or lesbian?" "How much time do you spend with this person now?" "Did their sexuality have any effect on your relationship?") allowed me to move beyond single variables of social contact or friendship.

Interview times ranged from approximately fifteen minutes to almost two hours in length. Typically, those with more conservative views about sexuality took a much longer time explaining their beliefs and attitudes. Interviewees who were most supportive of gay and lesbian rights finished their interviews more quickly and generally spent far less time explaining their religious beliefs and attitudes. For instance, the interview that only lasted fifteen minutes was with one of the most supportive respondents, who felt that the answers to my questions about rights were obvious and did not really need to even be discussed. Each respondent signed an informed consent form and agreed to have the interviews recorded.

Interviews were systematically coded with the use of qualitative data management software (MaxQDA). Each interview was transcribed in full and analyzed using existing theories of social contact theory and subcultural identity theory as sensitizing concepts. I began analysis using a number of sensitizing concepts, including social contact with gay and lesbian people, theological beliefs, beliefs about homosexuality, and beliefs about gay and lesbian civil rights. After coding interview responses into initial sensitizing concepts, I move to more nuanced axial coding. In addition, I paid close attention for emergent themes (themes that had not been anticipated).

Limitations

As with any project, there are some limitations to this study that should be pointed out. First, the difference between phone and face-to-face interviews should be considered. Nineteen of the interviews were completed face-to-face; twenty-one were conducted via telephone. Two limitations arise from this variation, the first being the influence of the researcher. While I attempted to present myself as neutral as possible in both dress and expression, there is always an influence between individuals when talking face-to-face. From my participants' responses, it seemed that each assumed I was similar to themselves in sexuality, religious beliefs, and attitudes toward homosexuality and gay and lesbian civil rights. The second limitation that could potentially arise due to these different types of interviews is my interpretation of what the respondents said. With the nineteen face-to-face interviews, I was able to read facial expressions and other nonverbal cues that would be missed in phone interviews. Despite these differences and limitations, respondents' answers were similar and consistent with the categories I presented in this study whether they were received face-to-face or via telephone.

Another limitation was the challenging tasks of gathering a sample of Mississippi churches and Christians willing to discuss religion and homosexuality. I recommend future researchers take time to develop relationships with more pastors and priests and congregations in order to gather larger samples. The conservative nature of the South, combined with the current framing of evangelical Protestants as homophobic and closed-minded, made it difficult to recruit conservative Christians who were willing to speak with an academic about sexuality. One way to overcome this limitation is through building rapport with conservative Christians. Trust is paramount for studying this topic, especially since evangelical Protestants have a high level of fear surrounding homosexuality and how they are framed in the media. Therefore, scholars and activists alike must continue to listen and understand the diversity within Christianity if we want to gain access to this population and truly understand their beliefs and attitudes.

Acknowledgments

First and foremost, I would like to thank my family and friends. I want to thank my wife, Sarah, who supports me in everything I do and who helped me edit this book. Thank you to my mom, dad, sister, grandmother, and other family members who struggled to make sense of my sexual identity and figure out a way to fit it into their worldview. I thank them for choosing love and acceptance; for choosing to accept me as I am rather than ostracize me based on one aspect of my identity. It is through their love, understanding, and acceptance that I am where I am today and am able to share this story and research. In addition to my family of origin, I am thankful for my chosen family—my friends. My friends have stood by me in times of happiness and struggle. I have been lucky to have great friends who have supported me through coming out and also throughout this project.

I would also like to thank my mentors for encouraging me and helping to make this project a reality. Thank you to Kimberly Kelly for your excellent mentorship and support throughout my PhD program and the writing of this book. Thank you to Nicole Rader, Lindsey Peterson, and Rachel Allison for your help with this project and so much more during my time as a graduate student at Mississippi State University. Thank you to Robert Freymeyer for sparking my love for sociology and my interest in this research. Thank you to Sarah Brauner-Otto for supporting my first study of this topic and coauthoring my first academic publication. Thank you to the Marion T. Loftin Dissertation Research Grant Committee at Mississippi State University for providing the funding to collect these data. Finally, thank you to John Bartkowski and the other anonymous reviewers who helped me improve the quality of this book for publication.

Last, but surely not least, I owe my sincere gratitude to the Mississippi Christians who took the time to complete the survey and participate in the interviews. Although I may not agree with many of my participants, I respect their honest opinions and willingness to share them with me. I genuinely hope this work portrays the respondents in this study in a fair light, and I hope that their experience with this project helped them to grow as much as it helped me.

Notes

Introduction

1. The painting represented the story of Noah, who God instructed to build a huge ark and to load aboard two of each type of all the animals in the world. The purpose was to save creation from a massive flood that God was sending due to the sins of humankind. At the end of the story, a rainbow appears to let Noah know that the flood is over and that God has saved him. This story is told in the book of Genesis, chapters 5–10.

2. I use the term homosexuality in this book because it is the term that many Christians continue to use. It is important to note that this term is no longer an acceptable label for individuals (unless someone personally states that this is how they identify). The term homosexuality has many negative connotations for the LGBTQ community. This is largely related to the medicalization of the term—the labeling of homosexuality as a medical disorder. Although homosexuality has not been listed as a mental disorder by the American Psychiatric Association in the Diagnostic and Statistical Manual of Mental Disorders since 1973, this historical labeling has led to much stigma around the term.

3. The forty interviewees were selected from a sample of Mississippi Christians who completed surveys, on which they indicated they had gay or lesbian friends or family members and were willing to participate in an interview.

4. While mainline Protestants in Mississippi (and the South more generally) align their theological beliefs more closely with evangelical Protestants than do mainline Protestants in other areas of the country, there remain distinct differences in beliefs about religion and homosexuality

between those who attend evangelical Protestant congregations and those who attend mainline Protestant congregations.

5. All but one of the congregations that agreed to let me sample from their members were predominantly white churches. Of the interviewees, all respondents except for three mainline Protestants and one evangelical Protestant identified as white. Therefore, an analysis of race is beyond the scope of this study. I do, however, provide the race of the participant speaking throughout the study.

6. Mainline Protestants make up 12 percent of respondents, compared to about 15 percent of American Christians more generally.

7. "Religious freedom bills" refers to a variety of bills proposed around the United States by Christians with the stated purpose of protecting Christians from punishment if they refuse services or rights to individuals based on their own religious beliefs. For example, these bills could include refusing a marriage license to same-sex couple or refusing to serve a same-sex couple in a restaurant if this is contrary to one's religious beliefs.

8. Many conservative Christians use the term "lifestyle" when discussing homosexuality. This term implies that gay and lesbian people choose being gay as a way of life. This is especially important because research indicates that if Christians feel being gay or lesbian is a choice, they are more likely to hold negative views against gay and lesbian people (Whitley 2009). In this study, some conservative Christians specifically referred to homosexuality as a "lifestyle" or "lifestyle of sin."

9. I use the phrases *same-sex marriage* and *same-sex adoption* throughout this study, rather than gay marriage or gay adoption, for a number of reasons. First, everyone involved in same-sex marriages or adoptions may not identify as gay or lesbian; they could identify as bisexual, asexual, or something else. Second, and relatedly, these phrases are more readily accepted by LGBTQ activists today. This is largely because the phrasing is more inclusive and removes some of the historical stigma surrounding the "gay marriage" or "gay adoption." Finally, using *gay*, the term generally defined as men who are physically or emotionally attracted to other men, as an all-encompassing term for everyone who is not heterosexual points to the sexist history of using the masculine as the default in our society.

1. God Said Love Thy Neighbor, Unless They're Gay

1. Participants are classified based on their denominational affiliations. For this study, evangelical Protestants are those who attend nondenominational Protestant churches, Lutheran churches, and/or Baptist churches. It must be noted, though, that there are nondenominational, Lutheran, and Baptist churches in the United States that are not identified as evangelical. In this study, however, those affiliated with these denominations were part of evangelical branches/churches based on the Pew Forum on Religious and Public Life's 2008 classification system.

2. Participants who identify as United Methodist, Presbyterian, or Episcopalian are considered mainline Protestants based on the Pew Forum's classification system.

3. All Catholics in this study were classified into one category, but there are some clear distinctions between liberal and conservative Catholics' beliefs and ideology.

2. For the Bible (or My Pastor/Priest) Tells Me So: The Bible and Homosexuality

1. The NIV translation of verse 5 reads, "They called to Lot, 'Where are the men who have came to you tonight? Bring them out to us so that we can have sex with them.'" The NABRE translation is the same as the NIV but uses the phrase "sexual relations" instead of sex.

2. The NIV translation of Leviticus 18:22 reads, "Do not have sexual relations with a man as one does with a woman; that is detestable." Similarly, Leviticus 20:13 in the NIV translation uses the word detestable, instead of abomination. The NABRE translation of Leviticus 20:13 reads, "If a man lies with a male as with a woman, they have committed an abomination; the two of them shall be put to death; their bloodguilt is upon them."

3. Even the Bible itself raises questions about the antigay interpretation of the story of Sodom and Gomorrah; see Ezekiel 16:49–50.

4. Some more progressive evangelical groups, such as the Sojourners, are affirming of gay and lesbian people and do not interpret these scriptures in the same condemning way.

5. NIV translation of Romans 1:26: "Because of this, God gave them over to shameful lusts. Even their women exchanged natural sexual relations for unnatural ones." NABRE translation of Romans 1:26: "Therefore, God handed them over to degrading passions. Their females exchanged natural relations for unnatural."

6. The NIV reads, "nor men who have sex with men," while the NABRE reads, "nor boy prostitutes" rather than "nor effeminate, nor abusers of themselves with mankind."

7. The NIV translation reads, "for the sexually immoral, for those practicing homosexuality, for slave traders . . ." and NABRE translation reads, "the unchaste, sodomites, kidnappers . . ."

3. Marriage = 1 Man + 1 Woman? Support and Opposition to Same-Sex Marriage

1. Two evangelical Protestant interviewees did indicate they would support same-sex marriage because marriage no longer has any meaning in our society and the government does not have the right to stop it.

2. Matthew 7:1; NIV translation.

5. All [Wo]men Are Created Equal, Or Are They? The Gay and Lesbian Civil Rights Movement

1. Nevertheless, the extreme negative attitudes toward this movement continue to be held primarily by evangelical Protestants.

2. For more details on the riots and movement, see Carter 2010; Duberman 1994; and Faderman 2016.

3. For a more comprehensive list of gay and lesbian civil rights milestones, see CNN's "LGBT Rights Milestones Fast Facts" 2018.

4. As a point of clarification, gay, lesbian, and bisexual individuals are more likely to live in poverty in the United States than are heterosexual people, as confirmed in a study by the Williams Institute (Badgett, Durso, and Schneebaum 2013).

6. Some of My Best Friends Are Gay: The Influence of Social Contact

1. In a meta-analysis of studies measuring the effects of social contact, Pettigrew and Tropp (2006) found social contact reduced prejudice in 94 percent of studies, making this a highly supported theory.

2. "Friend" and "family member" were defined by the respondent. I asked interviewees to discuss their friends and family members who identify as gay or lesbian and allowed them to determine what that means to them.

3. A master status is an individual's primary status that overrides all other statuses (Hughes 1945). The master status influences how people see the world and interact with it.

4. One evangelical respondent in the "Homosexuality is an Abomination" category stated that she supported gay and lesbian civil rights, but this was only because she did not believe the government should interfere with marriage and adoption. Her answers clearly displayed prejudice against gay and lesbian people and indicated that she held homosexuality to be sinful.

5. Cognitive dissonance occurs when people feel psychological discomfort when faced with two conflicting realities (Festinger 1957; Mahaffy 1996). If a Christian is faced with the reality of having a close friend or family member who identifies as gay or lesbian, while simultaneously practicing a religion that condemns same-sex relationships, this could lead to psychological discomfort.

References

Allport, Gordon W. 1954. *The Nature of Prejudice*. Boston: Addison-Wesley.

Annie E. Casey Foundation. 2014. "Twenty-Fifth Edition of KIDS COUNT Data Book Highlights Improvements in Health, Safety, Education and Decline in Teen Birth Rate since 1990." http://www.aecf.org/m/databook/2014KC_newsrelease_MS.pdf.

————. 2017. "2017 KIDS COUNT Data Book States Trends in Child Well-Being." http://www.aecf.org/m/resourcedoc/aecf-2017kidscountdatabook.pdf#page=43.

Badgett, M. V. Lee, Laura E. Durso, and Alyssa Schneebaum. 2013. "New Patterns of Poverty in the Lesbian, Gay, and Bisexual Community." Williams Institute. June. http://williamsinstitute.law.ucla.edu/research/census-lgbt-demographics-studies/lgbt-poverty-update-june-2013/#sthash.UZnpzsRT.dpuf.

Baker, Ashley A., and Sarah Brauner-Otto. 2015. "My Friend is Gay, But . . . : The Effects of Social Contact on Christian Evangelicals' Beliefs about Gays and Lesbians." *Review of Religious Research* 57, no. 2 (June): 239–268.

Bartkowski, John P. 1996. "Beyond Biblical Literalism and Inerrancy: Conservative Protestants and the Hermeneutic Interpretation of Scripture." *Sociology of Religion* 57, no. 3 (September): 259–272.

————. 2001. *Remaking the Godly Marriage: Gender Negotiation in Evangelical Families*. New Brunswick, N.J.: Rutgers University Press.

————. 2004. *The Promise Keepers: Servants, Soldiers, and Godly Men*. New Brunswick, N.J.: Rutgers University Press.

Bartkowski, John P., and Jen'nan Ghazal Read. 2003. "Veiled Submission: Gender, Power, and Identity among Evangelical and Muslim Women in the United States." *Qualitative Sociology* 26, no. 1 (March): 71–92.

Bartkowski, John P., and Helen A. Regis. 2003. *Charitable Choices: Religion, Race, and Poverty in the Post-welfare Era*. New York: New York University Press.

Barton, Bernadette. 2012. *Pray the Gay Away: The Extraordinary Lives of Bible Belt Gays*. New York: New York University Press.

Baruch, Yehuda, and Brooks C. Holtom. 2008. "Survey Response Rate Levels and Trends in Organization Research." *Human Relations* 61, no. 8 (August): 1139–1160.

Baunach, Dawn M., Elisabeth O. Burgess, and Courtney S. Muse. 2010. "Southern (Dis)comfort: Sexual Prejudice and Contact with Gay Men and Lesbians in the South." *Sociological Spectrum* 30, no. 1: 30–64.

Bramlett, Brittany H. 2012. "The Cross-Pressures of Religion and Contact with Gay/Lesbian People, and Their Impact on Same-Sex Marriage Opinion." *Politics & Policy* 40, no. 1 (February): 13–42.

Brasher, Brenda. 1998. *Godly Women: Fundamentalism and Female Power*. New Brunswick, N.J.: Rutgers University Press.

Butler, Judith. 1990. *Gender Trouble: Feminism and the Subversion of Identity*. New York: Routledge.

Carter, David. 2010. *Stonewall: The Riots That Sparked the Gay Revolution*. New York: St. Martin's.

CNN. 2010. "Americans Split Evenly on Gay Marriage." CNN. Accessed August 11. http://politicalticker.blogs.cnn.com/2010/08/11/americans -split-evenly-on-gay-marriage/.

———. 2018. "LGBT Rights Milestones Fast Facts." CNN. Accessed August 17. https://www.cnn.com/2015/06/19/us/lgbt-rights-milestones -fast-facts/index.html.

Collins, Patricia Hill. 1986. "Learning from the Outsider Within: The Sociological Significance of Black Feminist Thought." *Social Problems* 33, no. 6 (December): 14–32.

Connell, R. W., and James W. Messerschmidt. 2005. "Hegemonic Masculinity: Rethinking the Concept." *Gender & Society* 19, no. 6 (December): 829–859.

Coontz, Stephanie. 1992. *The Way We Never Were: American Families and the Nostalgia Trap*. New York: Basic Books.

D'Antonio, William V., Michele Dillon, and Mary L. Gautier. 2013. *American Catholics in Transition*. Lanham, Md.: Rowman & Littlefield.

Dey, Eric L. 1997. "Working with Low Survey Response Rates: The Efficacy of Weighing Adjustments." *Research in Higher Education* 38, no. 2 (April): 215–227.

Docter, Richard F., and Virginia Prince. 1997. "Transvestism: A Survey of 1032 Cross-Dressers." *Archives of Sexual Behavior* 26, no. 6 (December): 589–605.

Domonoske, Camila. 2016. "Mississippi Governor Signs 'Religious Freedom' Bill into Law." National Public Radio. Accessed April 5. http://www.npr .org/sections/thetwo-way/2016/04/05/473107959/mississippi-governor -signs-religious-freedom-bill-into-law.

Drake, Bruce. 2013. "As More Americans Have Contacts with Gay/Lesbian People, Social Acceptance Rises." Pew Research Center. Accessed June 18. http://www.pewresearch.org/fact-tank/2013/06/18/as-more -americans-have-contacts-with-gays-and-lesbians-social-acceptance -rises/.

Duberman, Martin Bauml. 1994. *Stonewall*. New York: Plume.

Duck, Robert J., and Bruce Hunsberger. 1999. "Religious Orientation and Prejudice: The Role of Religious Proscription, Right-Wing." *International Journal for the Psychology of Religion* 9, no. 3 (November): 157–179.

Emerson, Michael O., and Christian Smith. 2000. *Divided by Faith: Evangelical Religion and the Problem of Race in America*. New York: Oxford University Press.

Erzen, Tanya. 2006. *Straight to Jesus: Sexual and Christian Conversions in the Ex-gay Movement*. Berkeley: University of California Press.

Faderman, Lillian. 2016. *The Gay Revolution: The Story of the Struggle*. New York: Simon & Schuster.

Festinger, Leon. 1957. *A Theory of Cognitive Dissonance*. Palo Alto, Calif.: Stanford University Press.

Fetner, Tina. 2001. "Working Anita Bryant: The Impact of Christian Antigay Activism on Lesbian and Gay Movement Claims." *Social Problems* 48, no. 3 (August): 411–428.

———. 2008. *How the Religious Right Shaped Lesbian and Gay Activism*. Minnesota: University of Minnesota Press.

Freedom to Marry. 2018a. "The Freedom to Marry in Mississippi." Freedom to Marry. Accessed September 5, 2018. http://www.freedomtomarry.org/ states/mississippi.

———. 2018b. "Winning the Freedom to Marry Nationwide: The Inside Story of a Transformative Campaign." Freedom to Marry. Accessed September 5, 2018. http://www.freedomtomarry.org/pages/how-it-happened.

Gallagher, Sally K. 2003. *Evangelical Identity and Gendered Family Life.* New Brunswick, N.J.: Rutgers University Press.

———. 2004. "The Marginalization of Evangelical Feminism." *Sociology of Religion* 65, no. 3 (Autumn): 215–237.

Gallagher, Sally K., and Christian Smith. 1999. "Symbolic Traditionalism and Pragmatic Egalitarianism: Contemporary Evangelicals, Families, and Gender." *Gender & Society* 13, no. 2 (April): 211–233.

Gallup. 2018. "Marriage." Accessed September 5, 2018. https://news.gallup.com/poll/117328/marriage.aspx.

Gates, Gary J. 2013. "LGBT Parenting in the United States." Williams Institute. Accessed February 1. https://williamsinstitute.law.ucla.edu/research/census-lgbt-demographics-studies/lgbt-parenting-in-the-united-states/.

Gay Pride Calendar. 2017. "Pride Events." Accessed July 1. http://www.gaypridecalendar.com/byname.

Goffman, Erving. 1963. *Stigma: Notes on the Management of Spoiled Identity.* Upper Saddle River, N.J.: Prentice-Hall.

Griffith, R. Marie. 1997. *God's Daughters: Evangelical Women and the Power of Submission.* Palo Alto: University of California Press.

Gross, Larry P. 2001. *Up from Invisibility: Lesbians, Gay Men, and the Media in America.* New York: Columbia University Press.

Hankins, Barry. 2008. *American Evangelicals: A Contemporary History of a Mainstream Religious Movement.* Lanham, Md.: Rowman & Littlefield.

Haraway, Donna. 1988. "Situated Knowledges: The Science Question in Feminism and the Privilege of Partial Perspective." *Feminist Studies* 14, no. 3 (Autumn): 575–599.

Hart, Kylo-Patrick R. 2000. "Representing Gay Men on American Television." *Journal of Men's Studies* 9, no. 1 (October): 59–79.

Herek, Gregory M. 2000. "The Psychology of Sexual Prejudice." *Current Directions in Psychological Science* 9, no. 1 (February): 19–22.

———. 2011. "Anti-equality Marriage Amendments and Sexual Stigma." *Journal of Social Issues* 67, no. 2 (June): 413–426.

Hill, Eric D., Heather K. Terrell, Adam B. Cohen, and Craig T. Nagoshi. 2010. "The Role of Social Cognition in the Religious Evangelicalism-Prejudice Relationship." *Journal for the Scientific Study of Religion* 49, no. 4 (December): 724–739.

Hinrichs, Donald W., and Pamela J. Rosenberg. 2002. "Attitudes toward Gay, Lesbian, and Bisexual Persons among Heterosexual Liberal Arts College Students." *Journal of Homosexuality* 43, no. 1: 61–84.

Hochschild, Arlie Russell. 2016. *Strangers in Their Own Land: Anger and Mourning on the American Right.* New York: New Press.

Hodson, Gordon, Hannah Harry, and Andrea Mitchell. 2009. "Independent Benefits of Contact and Friendship on Attitudes toward Homosexuals among Authoritarians and Highly Identified Heterosexuals." *European Journal of Social Psychology* 39, no. 4: 509–525.

Hogg, Michael A., and Dominic Abrams. 1988. *Social Identifications: A Social Psychology of Intergroup Relations and Group Processes.* London: Routledge.

Hogg, Michael A., Deborah J. Terry, and Katherine M. White. 1995. "A Tale of Two Theories: A Critical Comparison of Identity Theory with Social Identity Theory." *Social Psychology Quarterly* 58, no. 4 (December): 255–269.

Howard, John. 1999. *Men like That: A Southern Queer History.* Chicago: University of Chicago Press.

Hughes, Everett C. 1945. "Dilemmas and Contradictions of Status." *American Journal of Sociology* 50, no. 5 (March): 353–359.

Karimi, Faith. 2016. "U.S. Judge Lifts Ban on Adoption by Same-Sex Couples in Mississippi." CNN. Accessed April 1. http://www.cnn.com/2016/04/01/us/mississippi-overturns-ban-gay-adoptions/index.html.

Kelly, Kimberly. 2012. "In the Name of the Mother: Renegotiating Conservative Women's Authority in the Crisis Pregnancy Center Movement." *Signs* 38, no. 1 (September): 203–229.

Konieczny, Mary Ellen. 2013. *The Spirit's Tether: Family, Work, and Religion among American Catholics.* New York: Oxford University Press.

Lewis, Gregory B. 2011. "The Friends and Family Plan: Contact with Gays and Support for Gay Rights." *Policy Studies Journal* 39, no. 2 (May): 217–238.

Mahaffy, Kimberly A. 1996. "Cognitive Dissonance and Its Resolution: A Study of Lesbian Christians." *Journal for the Scientific Study of Religion* 35, no. 4 (December): 392–402.

Manning, Christel. 1999. *God Gave Us the Right: Conservative Catholic, Evangelical Protestant, and Orthodox Jewish Women Grapple with Feminism.* New Brunswick, N.J.: Rutgers University Press.

Marsh, Charles. 1997. *God's Long Summer: Stories of Faith and Civil Rights.* Princeton: Princeton University Press.

McQueeney, Krista. 2009. "'We Are God's Children, Y'all': Race, Gender, and Sexuality in Lesbian- and Gay-Affirming Congregations." *Social Problems* 56, no. 1 (February):151–173.

McVeigh, Rory, and Maria-Elena D. Diaz. 2009. "Voting to Ban Same-Sex Marriage: Interests, Values, and Communities." *American Sociological Review* 74, no. 6 (December): 891–915.

Newport, Frank. 2011. "For the First Time, Majority of Americans Favor Legal Gay Marriage." Gallup. Accessed May 20. http://www.gallup.com/poll/147662/first-time-majority-americans-favor-legal-gay-marriage.aspx.

Olson, Laura R., Wendy Cadge, and James T. Harrison. 2006. "Religion and Public Opinion about Same-Sex Marriage." *Social Science Quarterly* 87, no. 2 (June): 340–360.

Palmer, Emily, and Campbell Robertson. 2016. "Mississippi Fights to Keep Control of Its Beleaguered Child Welfare System." *New York Times.* Accessed January 17. https://www.nytimes.com/2016/01/18/us/mississippi-fights-to-keep-control-of-itsbeleaguered-child-welfare-system.html.

PBS. 2011. "How the Pride Parade Became Tradition." Accessed November 1, 2016. http://www.pbs.org/wgbh/americanexperience/blog/2011/06/09/pride-parade/.

Perry, Samuel L., and Andrew L. Whitehead. 2016. "Religion and Public Opinion toward Same-Sex Relations, Marriage, and Adoption: Does the Type of Practice Matter?" *Journal for the Scientific Study of Religion* 55, no. 3 (March): 637–651.

Peters, Stephen. 2016. "HRC Previews Anti-LGBT State and Local Legislation." Human Rights Campaign. Accessed January 8. http://www.hrc.org/blog/hrc-previews-anti-lgbt-state-local-legislation.

Pettigrew, Thomas F. 1998. "Intergroup Contact Theory." *Annual Reviews Psychology* 49: 65–85.

Pettigrew, Thomas F., and Linda R. Tropp. 2006. "A Meta-analytic Test of Intergroup Contact Theory." *Journal of Personality and Social Psychology* 90, no. 5 (May): 751–783.

Pettigrew, Thomas F., Linda R. Tropp, Ulrich Wagner, and Oliver Christ. 2011. "Recent Advances in Intergroup Contact Theory." *International Journal of Intercultural Relations* 35, no. 3 (May): 271–280.

Pew Forum on Religion and Public Life. 2008. Pew Research Center. Accessed February 1, 2008. "U.S. Religious Landscape Survey—Religious Affiliation: Diverse and Dynamic." http://www.pewforum.org/files/2013/ 05/report-religious-landscape-study-full.pdf.

———. 2014. "Religious Landscape Study." Pew Research Center. Accessed November 1, 2016. http://www.pewforum.org/religious-landscape-study/ #religions.

———. 2015. "America's Changing Religious Landscape: Christians Decline Sharply as Share of Population; Unaffiliated and Other Faiths Continue to Grow." Pew Research Center. Accessed May 12. http://www .pewforum.org/2015/05/12/americas-changing-religious-landscape/.

———. 2017. "Changing Attitudes on Gay Marriage." Pew Research Center. Accessed June 26. http://www.pewforum.org/fact-sheet/changing -attitudes-on-gay-marriage/.

Rowatt, Wade C., Jo-Ann Tsang, Jessica Kelly, Brooke LaMartina, Michelle McCullers, and April McKinley. 2006. "Associations between Religious Personality Dimensions and Implicit Homosexual Prejudice." *Journal for the Scientific Study of Religion* 45, no. 3 (August): 397–406.

Saucier, Donald A., and Audrey J. Cawman. 2004. "Civil Unions in Vermont: Political Attitudes, Religious Fundamentalism, and Sexual Prejudice." *Journal of Homosexuality* 48, no. 1: 1–18.

Sax, Linda J., Shannon K. Gilmartin, and Alyssa N. Bryant. 2003. "Assessing Response Rates and Nonresponse Bias in Web and Paper Surveys." *Research in Higher Education* 44, no. 4 (August): 409–432.

Schreiber, Ronnee. 2008. *Righting Feminism: Conservative Women and American Politics.* New York: Oxford University Press.

Sherkat, Darren E., Melissa Powell-Williams, Gregory Maddox, and Kylan Mattias de Vries. 2011. "Religion, Politics, and Support for Same-Sex Marriage in the United States, 1988–2008." *Social Science Research* 40, no. 1 (January): 167–180.

Shih, Tse-Hua, and Xitao Fan. 2009. "Comparing Response Rates in Email and Paper Surveys: A Meta-analysis." *Educational Research Review* 4, no. 1: 26–40.

Simon, Carolyn. 2013. "Reflecting on 10 Years since the Goodridge Decision Brought Marriage Equality to Massachusetts." Human Rights Campaign. Accessed November 18. https://www.hrc.org/blog/entry/reflecting -on-10-years-since-the-goodridge-decision-brought-marriage-equali.

Smith, Christian. 2000. *Christian America? What Evangelicals Really Want.* Palo Alto: University of California Press.

Smith, Christian, Michael Emerson, Sally Gallagher, Paul Kennedy, and David Sikkink. 1998. *American Evangelicalism: Embattled and Thriving.* Chicago: University of Chicago Press.

Smith, Dorothy E. 1987. *The Everyday World as Problematic: A Feminist Sociology.* Boston: Northeastern University Press.

Solnit, Rebecca. 2014. *Men Explain Things to Me.* Chicago: Haymarket Books.

Stets, Jan E., and Peter J. Burke. 2000. "Identity Theory and Social Identity Theory." *Social Psychology Quarterly* 63, no. 3 (September): 224–237.

Tan, Avianne. 2016. "Mississippi's 'Religious Freedom' Bill: What to Know about the New 'Sweeping Anti-LGBT Law.'" ABC News. Accessed April 6. http://abcnews.go.com/US/mississippis-religious-freedom-bill -sweeping-anti-lgbt-law/story?id=38170420.

Wellman, James K. 2008. *Evangelicals vs. Liberals: The Clash of Christian Cultures in the Pacific Northwest.* New York: Oxford University Press.

Whitley, Bernard E., Jr. 2009. "Religiosity and Attitudes toward Lesbians and Gay Men: A Meta-analysis." *International Journal for the Psychology of Religion* 19, no. 1 (January): 21–38.

Wilkinson, Wayne W. 2004. "Religiosity, Authoritarianism, and Homophobia: A Multidimensional Approach." *International Journal for the Psychology of Religion* 14, no. 1 (January): 55–67.

Zuberi, Tukufu, and Eduardo Bonilla-Silva. 2008. *White Logic, White Methods: Racism and Methodology.* Lanham, Md.: Rowman & Littlefield.

Zylstra, Sarah Eekhoff. 2014. "The Most Popular and Fastest Growing Bible Translation Isn't What You Think It Is." Christianity Today. Accessed March 13. http://www.christianitytoday.com/gleanings/2014/march/most -popular-and-fastest-growing-bible-translation-niv-kjv.html?paging=off.

Index

Page numbers in *italics* refer to figures.

in Bible passages, 64; judgment and, 131; in Mississippi, 11; opinion on other churches, 73; prejudices toward gays and lesbians, 24; religious identity and, 29; same-sex adoption and, 101, 103; same-sex marriage, opposition to, 86–89; same-sex marriage, support for, 90; secular society and, 157–158; social contact and, 129, 144, 145, 150–151, 153, 154, 159–160; in the South, 11; stereotypes of, 61, 163, 177; subcultural identity and, 29–30, 33, 86, 157–158; uncertainty about Bible, 66

Ezekiel, book of, 183n3 (chap. 2)

family: "Christian," 86; formation of, 39; nuclear, 28, 86, 101; single-parent, 101; traditional, 35, 36, 86, 92, 101, 109; traditional, gays and lesbians excluded from, 37

family members, gay and lesbian, 127, 151–152, 155; definitions of, 185n2; embarrassment about, 136–137; influence of, 13–14, 18; love for, 147, 148, 152

family values, 35, 38

femininity, 35, 41, 103, 104, 105, 135; in Bible, 65

feminism, 38, 40

First Corinthians, book of, 56, 57, 64; NABRE translation of, 184n6; NIV translation of, 184n6

First Timothy, book of, 56, 57, 64; NABRE translation of, 184n7; NIV translation of, 184n7

foster care system, 103, 108

Francis, Pope, 4, 24, 41

friends, gay and lesbian, 127, 150–151; definitions of, 185n2; embarrassment about, 136–137; influence of, 13–14, 18

fundamentalist Protestants, 3

Gallagher, Sally K., 37–38

gay and lesbian civil rights movement: as benefit to society, 115–116, 123; descriptors for, 112; fear of, 112, 124; as having mixed results for society, 116–117; history of, 110; lack of knowledge of, 117; in Mississippi, 165; opposition to, 111–115, 122; as outlandish, 119; as polarizing, 111; pride parades and, 118–119; as threat to individuals, 112; as threat to society, 111–115, 123

gay and lesbian equality, 110, 162; as excluding marriage, 85, 91; pride parades and, 118

gay and lesbian rights: attitudinal shift, 11; backlash against, 11–12; as boundary, 42; government and, 90, 184n1, 185n4; marriage not supported as, 85; in Mississippi, 13; religion as major opposition to, 83; as "special rights," 102, 114, 117; as threat, 30

gay pride parades, 117–120

gays and lesbians: church leadership and, 70–73; conditional acceptance of, 68–70, 71; devaluation of, 22; marginalization of, 11; in Mississippi, 12–13; priesthood and, 68; "saving" of, 62, 69, 81, 151

gender, 41–42; as boundary, 34–36, 38; expectations, 36; ideology of, 35, 37, 38, 42, 65; norms, 36, 40, 104; performance of, 35; practices, 37–38; roles, 35, 36, 40, 102–103; vs. sexuality, 65, 104, 135; subcultural identity and, 37

gender essentialism, 36, 101, 109

gender expression, 41, 135

Genesis, book of, 54–55, 181n1

God: defiance of, 87–88; falling away from, 89; as infallible, 48; judgment of, 22–23, 60–61

Goodridge et al. v. Department of Public Health, 83–84

Hankins, Barry, 36

hate, 11, 61–62, 81, 158

HB 1523 (Mississippi). *See* Religious Liberty Accommodations Act

Hebrews, book of, 59

hermeneutic circle, 47, 50, 60, 75

108; as sacrament, 94, 108; traditional, 94; use of term, 91; wholeness and, 37. *See also* same-sex marriage

Marsh, Charles, 165, 169

masculinity, 35, 41, 103, 104, 105, 135

Massachusetts, same-sex marriage and, 83–84

master status, 144, 149, 162, 185n3

Matthew, book of, 184n2

methodology, 171–177; ethics and, 44; interviews, 5, 174–176; location, 5; sampling, 171–172, 177; surveys, 172, 173–174

Mississippi, 11–13; as battleground state, 164–165; child welfare in, 108; opposition to mainstream, 34; same-sex adoption in, 100; single-parent families in, 101, 109; subculture of, 34

moral accountability, 29

NABRE. *See* New American Bible (Revised Edition)

natural law theology, 33, 34

negative features, 130–131, 149, 154

New American Bible (Revised Edition) (NABRE), 54

New International Version (NIV), 54, 56; translation of "homosexuality," 57

New Testament: Old Testament law and, 56, 58–59; passages on homosexuality, 53, 56–58, 63–65. *See also individual books*

NIV. *See* New International Version

nonjudgment, 3, 23, 61, 75, 155

Obergefell v. Hodges, 84

Old Testament: as obsolete, 58–60; passages on homosexuality, 53–56, 63–65. *See also individual books*

opposite-sex role models, 104, 105, 106

"other," 82–89, 164, 168

Paul, apostle, 57–59, 58, 63, 64

Pence, Mike, 167

Pettigrew, Thomas F., 128, 130, 139, 154

Phelps, Fred, 5

polarization, 32, 111, 166, 167

political Christian organizations, 113

polygamy, gay and lesbian rights as leading to, 87, 112

poverty, 108, 184n4

pragmatic egalitarianism, 38

prejudice, 24, 47, 49–50, 128, 139, 160

pride parades. *See* gay pride parades

procreation, 33, 39, 58, 66, 92–93

Protestants. *See* evangelical Protestants; mainline Protestants

religion: contradictions in, 83; as major argument against gay and lesbian rights, 62–74, 80, 83; as overshadowing relationships, 151, 154, 155, 159–160; prejudice and, 25–26; as "saving" gays and lesbians, 81; truth and, 24

"religious freedom bills," 12, 80, 167, 168, 182n7

Religious Liberty Accommodations Act (HB 1523, Mississippi), 12, 80, 100, 167

Religious Right, 35

Romans, book of, 56–57, 59, 64, 65; NABRE translation of, 184n5; NIV translation of, 184n5

same-sex adoption, 36, 96–97, 99–109, 182n9; as "better than nothing," 103–106; as civil institution, 109; as confusing children, 102–103, 105; fear of, 82; as harming children, 101–103; as more supported than same-sex marriage, 107–109; opposition to, 100–103; as redefining family, 101; restrictions on, 106; social contact and, 148; societal consequences of, 107; support for, 106–108

same-sex marriage, 84–98; as benefit to society, 95–97; vs. civil unions, 85, 91–95, 147–148; as defying God, 87; evangelical Protestant opposition to, 42; fear of, 82, 85; gender expectations and, 36; government and, 85, 184n1; history of, 83–84; legalization of, 111, 164;

About the Author

BAKER A. ROGERS is an assistant professor of sociology at Georgia Southern University. Their research focuses on inequality, specifically examining the intersections of gender, sexuality, religion, and geographical location. Their work has been published in *Gender & Society*, *Qualitative Sociology*, *Sexualities*, *Review of Religious Research*, and *Feminist Teacher*.